Wood Finishing Simplified

with Joe L'Erario

POPULAR WOODWORKING BOOKS

Cincinnati, Ohio
www.popularwoodworking.com

Read This
Important Safety Notice

To prevent accidents, keep safety in mind while you work. Use the safety guards installed on power equipment; they are for your protection. When working on power equipment, keep fingers away from saw blades, wear safety goggles to prevent injuries from flying wood chips and sawdust, wear hearing protection and consider installing a dust vacuum to reduce the amount of airborne sawdust in your woodshop. Don't wear loose clothing, such as neckties or shirts with loose sleeves, or jewelry, such as rings, necklaces or bracelets, when working on power equipment. Tie back long hair to prevent it from getting caught in your equipment. People who are sensitive to certain chemicals should check the chemical content of any product before using it. The authors and editors who compiled this book have tried to make the contents as accurate and correct as possible. Plans, illustrations, photographs and text have been carefully checked. All instructions, plans and projects should be carefully read, studied and understood before beginning construction. Due to the variability of local conditions, construction materials, skill levels, etc., neither the author nor Popular Woodworking Books assumes any responsibility for any accidents, injuries, damages or other losses incurred resulting from the material presented in this book. Prices listed for supplies and equipment were current at the time of publication and are subject to change.

Metric Conversion Chart

to convert	to	multiply by
Inches	Centimeters	2.54
Centimeters	Inches	0.4
Feet	Centimeters	30.5
Centimeters	Feet	0.03
Yards	Meters	0.9
Meters	Yards	1.1

Wood Finishing Simplified with Joe L'Erario Copyright ©2008 by Joe L'Erario. Printed and bound in China. All rights reserved. No part of this book may be reproduced in any form or by any electronic or mechanical means including information storage and retrieval systems without permission in writing from the publisher, except by a reviewer, who may quote brief passages in a review. Published by Popular Woodworking Books, an imprint of F+W Publications, Inc., 4700 East Galbraith Road, Cincinnati, Ohio, 45236. First edition.

Distributed in Canada by Fraser Direct
100 Armstrong Avenue
Georgetown, Ontario L7G 5S4
Canada

Distributed in the U.K. and Europe by David & Charles
Brunel House
Newton Abbot
Devon TQ12 4PU
England
Tel: (+44) 1626 323200
Fax: (+44) 1626 323319
E-mail: postmaster@davidandcharles.co.uk

Distributed in Australia by Capricorn Link
P.O. Box 704
Windsor, NSW 2756
Australia

Visit our Web site at www.popularwoodworking.com for information on more resources for woodworkers.

Other fine Popular Woodworking Books are available from your local bookstore or direct from the publisher.

12   11   10   09   08   5   4   3   2   1

Library of Congress Cataloging-in-Publication Data

L'Erario, Joe.
    Wood finishing simplified / with Joe L'Erari. -- 1st ed.
        p. cm.
    Includes index.
    ISBN 978-1-55870-807-5 (pbk. : alk. paper)
    1. Wood finishing. I. Title.
    TT325.L465 2008
    684'.08--dc22
                                                    2007048886

Acquisitions editor: David Thiel
Senior editor: Jim Stack
Cover designer: Terri Woesner
Interior layout: Amy F. Wilkin
Production coordinator: Mark Griffin
Photographer: Al Parrish

About the Author
Joe L'Erario

For ten years, Joe L'Erario was co-host of the television programs *Furniture on the Mend*, *Furniture to Go* and *Men in Toolbelts*. He has been finishing furniture since 1978 and has taught seminars on wood finishing and decorative finishes throughout North America. He is also coauthor of *The Furniture Guys Book* and most recently, *Creating the Perfect Wood Finish with Joe L'Erario*, published by Popular Woodworking books.

In addition, Joe is an artist who has been painting for as far back as he can remember. To view Joe's artwork you can log onto www.paintrunsdeep.com

Joe has a son Zane, from a previous marriage and lives in Ottawa, Ontario with his wife Heidi, three stepdaughters, a smart cat and two really, really dumb ones.

Acknowledgements

I'd like to thank, first and foremost, Jim Stack, for his belief, David Thiel for his assistance and Al Parrish for his great photos.

I'd also like to thank Ehren Katzur for his participation during the photo shoot (man hitting himself with a hammer pg. 39), my agent, Art Miller, because he makes me laugh (you're the best, Art!) and Steve Higgins for the extra photos.

Most of all, to my wonderful "Catchy," yes, my wife Heidi, because, well, I couldn't do any of this without you. You make me spin babe! I love you all.

contents

introduction

Just who is this book for?

I ask you: Who better than a simpleton to author a book with this title?

This is a guidebook for the novice. It is a book that deals with strict basics utilizing materials that are readily available from the home center or local (well-stocked) hardware store. So, if you're nodding your head in agreement — like, finally, there's-a-book-for-me kind of nod — consider that I wrote it with you in mind. Also, if you are looking for a book that's going to give you a heads up on every possible method, idea and product in the finishing world, may I suggest the latest absorbing Larry King (written "with") crime novel instead?

The long and the short of it is, this book is going to help you to create simple, lasting finishes on things you've spent hours making. And when I say "simple," understand that I don't for a moment mean easy, right-out-of-the-can simple. Do you get what I'm saying? I mean, if you want no-fuss no-muss results you will just have to check out the infomercial of your choice and send in your money — and please let me know how the product worked for you.

I'm not advocating this book as being better than another, only that its direction is aimed at you — the amateur woodworker.

Becoming acquainted with the materials involved and their methods of application may try your patience, however, once mastered, you will find that it will take less time for you to create a finish of lasting beauty on your work than you may have thought possible.

I also encourage you to visit a well-stocked art supply store for a few items that you won't be able to locate at the home center. (Relax. A beret is not one of these items.)

As a novice beginning with the basics there are a few other specialty items you may or may not wish to acquire through mail order or over the Internet, depending on how adventurous or enthusiastic you become, and, if it's okay by you, I will touch upon these items as we move along.

The one thing I will guarantee is that, in a short while, you may find yourself finishing furniture like a pro — or even writing a book!

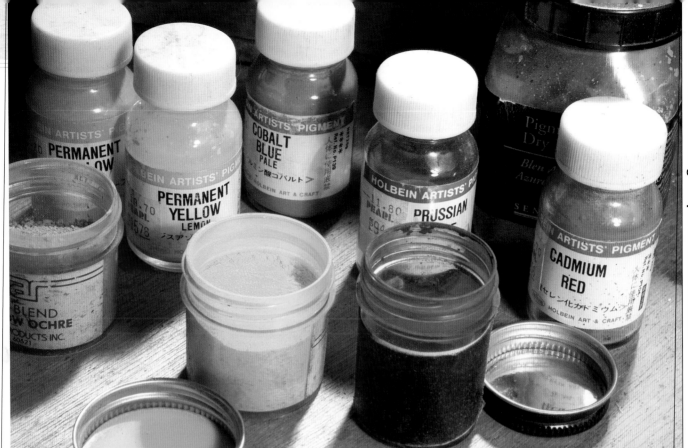

★You and your finish

You are about to take part in a great adventure. Well, maybe not all that great, but quite informative. Come along with me through the aisles and I'll point out some of the many things essential to the art of finishing, refinishing and general painting. And, along the way, I'll try to clear up some of the mysteries surrounding various assorted items while bumping into any number of things and hurting myself.

Starting at finishing

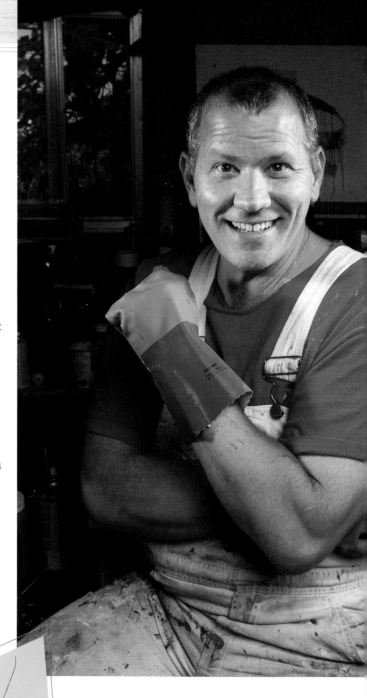

The mindset of most amateur furniture makers and wood-workers who set out to learn wood finishing by reading a book is to look for something that's going to give them insight. What they are often confronted with, however, can be overly challenging. It would be like trying to cook a five-star French meal and comprehending a James Beard cookbook without ever having seen a cookbook, let alone knowing what a bouquet garnish is — or who James Beard is for that matter.

It is my opinion, given that I have taught numerous wood-working seminars on just the stuff this book's about, that what novice woodworkers crave is instruction on that perfect, most simple finish, because, well, let's face it, those of you who build stuff give little thought as to how you want the wood to look afterward. So, when it comes time to apply finish, you wind up slapping anything on the wood and calling it a day.

Am I right?

This is caused by either a slight indifference to wood finishing (as if it was beneath you), or, a fear of a product. Yet you continue to run out and buy something called a guidebook, expecting to gain the knowledge that will give you the power to enact miracles on your project without even knowing the basics.

I think it's safe for me to say that most of you out there expect miracles to happen the moment you get back to your workshop while following along with a recipe in a book, especially if that book describes things that you aren't even able to purchase at a home center or local hardware store. Am I right again?

Well, I know the feeling.

I was there some 29 years ago. I know that all-consuming need for instant results. Would that magic wands were available next to the paintbrushes at the hardware store, eh?

Personally, I feel that most finishing books are crammed with way too much information for beginners. At times, information may be too overloaded or way too advanced or technical — not to mention way too scientific with graphs and chemical breakdowns of paints and varnishes that can make you absolutely nutty.

I can look through these kinds of books and always derive something from their pages because I already know the basics and have been doing stuff with most of the products mentioned in most finishing books for some time now. Mostly I can honestly say I look through these books to see if the authors have made any mistakes, or, if I have been making any mistakes in the way that I do things. In any case, it's all research. Welcome to the club.

I've been in the business of finishing and refinishing furniture and anything else made of wood for about 29 years now, and have suffered through what may seriously be referred to as living nightmares. In all that time, I don't believe I have ever taken the time to ponder what makes it so easy for me to do what I do. This is precisely why you are holding this book in your hands. (By the way, if you've gotten this far in the text, why don't you go and pay for the book already and read the rest in the comfort of your own home?)

Because wood finishing is second nature to me, I never give it a second thought. And, my friends, let me tell you, I've been perplexed by many a hair-pulling situation — which, in case you hadn't noticed, is why I am bald on top.

Over the many years I have been in the business, I have had to overcome and solve many problems with finishes I and others have applied: mysterious appearances of air-bubbles, pock marks, varieties of dust bumps, scratches, dings, cracking, stains bleeding through, parts missing and needing to be duplicated — not to mention the agonizing around-the-clock babying of finishes curing in improper temperatures. I can remember worrying that storm clouds were going to appear in my shop once the moist heat of a sweltering summer day became friendly with my air-conditioning.

I have been through it all — even to the point of working out of established businesses whose proprietors may have hired me to solve a problem and then would not allow me to solve the problem they hired me to solve simply because they didn't want to stray from the norm of how they went about applying their finishes! If I'd suggest a brushed-on, superior (in every way) varnish, whose durability was a proven fact over common nitrocellulose lacquer — especially where a table surface might be concerned — it would have them scratching their chins, wrinkling their brows, clearing their throats. They were so unfamiliar with the act of brushing material onto wood that they just didn't want to take the chance.

If I think back to when I first started learning — when curiosity was my main drive — to my most present troubling situation with a finish, I realize that the answer is as basic as it is simple:

The more you do something of a repetitive nature, the easier it gets.

No more than this.

However, you must have the curiosity to begin with, otherwise, you are simply following recipes. Now understand, this is fine if you want to be a recipe follower, but at some point you must forget the stuff you've written on index cards or in notebooks and wing it.

Listen, and this is from the horse's mouth:

Any information you acquire as you learn more and more on wood finishing, product compatibility and any learned techniques you may master, will automatically become second nature for you.

Knowing this, I began to think about those first basic steps I myself took back in 1978, and for the heck of it, I began titling chapters of, say, a cookbook that would purport to cover similar kinds of basics in the vast field of cooking. For instance: Boiling Water. What is a Knife? And what about, Pushing the Toaster Button Downwards? I think you will agree that you can't get anymore basic than this.

In my world, applying a full shellac finish (see Chapter 4, Simple shellac and wax) of three to six coats in a single day on new wood, or on wood that I've stripped, while managing a meal for five, is as simple as boiling water!

Know thy stuff

Shellac. Varnish. Lacquer. Polyurethane. These are common words to the novice ear. We know each is used as top-coating material: Thick, clear, or semiclear liquids that may either be brushed or sprayed onto wood to beautify as well as protect.

But what about pumice? Ketones? Petroleum distillates? Toluene? Xylene? Denatured Alcohol? Acetone? Oxalic acid? Yikes!

These and other product or solvent names are recurrent in the field of wood finishing, basic to the chore, yet remain as unclear and undecipherable as cuneiform to people who do not know any better.

And why should you know about these things anyway? As my wife is always so keen to say to me when I am stumped: "What good is banging your head against the wall? No one is born with the knowledge y'know?" And she's absolutely right. You have to seek, you have to ask questions, and, if you're like me, you repair a lot of walls.

That's why discussing labels on the back of cans and bottles is important. Knowing specific ingredients will allow you to make better choices and avoid making mistakes. If you do not know what solvent is compatible with your finish you are asking for trouble. As you get better at deciphering labels, the nose takes over and it is through the good old schnoz that you will be able to decipher the mysteries of chemical (product) compatibility.

For example, let me tell you about the time a guy came to my shop bearing the top from a Victrola from the 1920s. (Those of you out there over forty may know what a Victrola is, those of you who deal in Ipods and steal from the Internet probably don't even care, but I will tell you anyway.)

A Victrola is an old-fashioned record player. (If you do know not what a record is, I give up.) They were usually constructed from oak or mahogany and finished with shellac. Believe it or not, they were as widespread and as popular as today's personal listening systems are — although you'd be hard-pressed to carry them around with you let alone attach wires to your ears for the music to travel through.

You would wind up the "machine," as my grandmother used to called it, using the crank on the side panel. This spun the turntable. Upon placing the heavy needle onto the record, you would be able to listen to, say, Caruso, who, at the time, was as popular as Michael Bublé — but with talent.

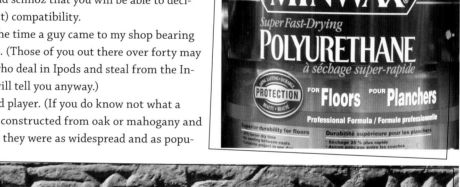

Enrico Caruso

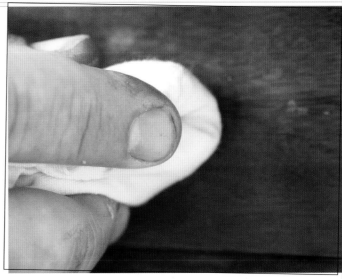

Anyway, what this guy had done was splatter white paint on the top of his grandfather's 1920s quarter-sawn oak Victrola. He told me a few hours had passed before he'd noticed what had happened so the paint had already begun to set up. In a panic, he told me he had tried wiping the paint from the surface using a popular spray cleaner of the time.

This was back when there were maybe three or four major spray cleaners on the shelves of supermarkets, unlike today where you can choose from 32 different designer-colored spray cleaners just for glass! Armed with his spray and his rag, he rubbed frantically to get the paint from the surface.

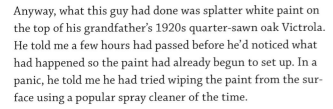

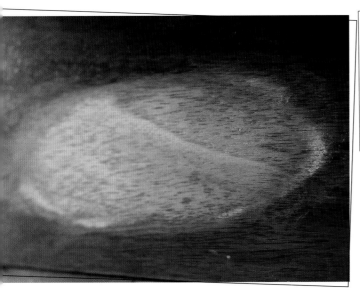

He rubbed so well he went clean down to the wood and left a spot.

Now why would this happen you may ask. Well, I'll tell you: Many home spray cleaners, then as well as now, contain ammonia, and ammonia will dissolve shellac — it will also revive you after you've passed out!

The plain truth of the matter is, and what I'm trying to get across to you is, had the guy known this basic fact, he would have avoided the aggravation and saved himself a hundred and fifty bucks to boot — which is what I charged him to restore the top.

The solvents

First, understand that solvents can be dangerous. They can cause headaches, various skin and eye irritations and, need I even say it, fires.

Don't believe for a minute that one solvent is less dangerous than another. Always take precautions when using these and other products, otherwise, you may be finished before you even get to finishing.

Of the many solvents that make up various removers, stains, paint, and top coatings, there are really only a few that you need to be able to identify immediately. You can accomplish this by simply identifying the listed names on the backs of bottle and cans, and later, when you are adept at recognizing scents, you will be able to differentiate through the glorious sense of smell and you will instinctively know what may be mixed with what.

I remember a Three Stooges routine where Curly drinks some paint from a cup he thinks is his coffee. When he discovers what he's drank isn't his coffee, he goes into his "Woo, woo, woo" routine, while Larry, in an effort to save his chum, reacts quickly and says: "Hold it! I'll fix it," and gives him some paint remover to drink. To, ah, err, well, remove the paint. Get it? Nyuk, nyuk.

I knew about paint removers, paints, and thinners from the time I was six or seven because my father used them all the time. There was always some kind of transformation going on in my little row home in South Philadelphia back in the early 1960s when old timers such as my dad stuck to oil-based paints — and the entire house would smell like a pine forest from his reservoir of turpentine. Keep in mind that even then I knew not to drink the stuff because my father had smacked me in the head one day and said, "Don't drink the stuff!" (Well, okay, he may have hollered it.) Not that I ever would have tried, mind you. It was just his particular method of teaching.

So there you have it. Like my father before me, I'm telling you, okay? Don't drink the stuff! (I'm letting you know this because none of the labels you are going to see accompanying my text is going to say "drink a lot while using."

When you refer to paint thinners, there are about six that should concern us: acetone, mineral spirits, turpentine, naphtha, toluene and xylene. All of these can be used in the reduction and thinning of certain paints, enamels, stains and varnishes, but you have to know which are better suited for your particular needs.

3.78 Litres

Pure Turpentine
Térébenthine pure

the professional's choice for thinning varnishes, paints and enamels; for cleaning surfaces and brushes.
Le choix des professionnels pour éclaircir les peintures, vernis et émaux;

CONTENTS HARMFUL. CONTENTS MAY CATCH FIRE. Do not swallow. Keep out of reach children. Wear a mask. Do not smoke. Use only in a well-ventilated area. Keep away from flames, such as a pilot light and any object that sparks, such as an electric motor. To open - hold tab against cap and turn counter clockwise. To close - turn cap clockwise until tight.
FIRST AID TREATMENT: Contains Turpentine. If swallowed, call a Poison Control Centre or doctor immediately. If person is alert, do not induce vomiting, product can be aspirated into lungs.
CONTENU NOCIF. LE CONTENU PEUT S'ENFLAMMER. Ne pas avaler. Tenir hors de la portée des enfants. Porter un masque. Ne pas fumer. N'utiliser que dans un endroit bien aéré. Tenir loin des flammes, telle une flamme pilote, et de tout objet produisant des étincelles, tel moteur électrique.
Pour ouvrir, tenir la languette contre la capsule et tourner en sens inverse des aiguilles d'une montre. Pour fermer, tourner et serrer la capsule dans le sens des aiguilles d'une montre.
PREMIERS SOINS : Contient de la térébenthine. En cas d'ingestion, appeler immédiatement un centre antipoison ou un médecin. Si la personne est consciente, ne pas provoque vomissement, le produit peut être aspiré dans les poumons.

Turpentine

Called spirits of turpentine (from the Greek word *terebinthine*, or *terebinth tree* from whose sap the spirit was first distilled), this solvent may also be called wood turpentine or gum turpentine. Turpentine is derived through the distillation of resin obtained from many different species of pine trees. During Colonial American times turpentine was called *rosin*. It was used in the manufacture of liniment ointments (chest rubs) and there are records indicating that some medical treatments even prescribed drinking the stuff — yech! I'd rather drink Postum! (Postum was a powdered coffee substitute sold by the Kraft Foods company.)

Turpentine has a strong odor and is another ingredient often added to cleaning products for that clean-smelling pine scent. As I told you, my Dad used it for painting. It was in the Pine-Sol he added to a bucket of water for mopping up the basement, and when I was sick he'd rub it on my chest in the form of Vicks VapoRub — cough!

Paint thinner (mineral spirits)

Many people don't know that mineral spirits and paint thinner, like Clark Kent and Superman, are one and the same. The container will either read paint thinner, and in parentheses state "mineral spirits," or, the other way around — mineral spirits "paint thinner." There are other names such as Varsol, which is the name under which it goes in Canada, eh?

But what we commonly refer to as paint thinner (mineral spirits) is a petroleum solvent distilled from crude oil and used as a turpentine substitute due to its less offensive smell. Art supply stores also carry an odorless paint thinner, but with a nose like mine I can still detect an odor to it. Paint thinner is used mainly as paint and varnish thinner, for cleaning rollers and brushes, removing splatters of paint from surfaces, hands and face, as a degreaser for industrial machinery parts and is a major ingredient of many insecticides — the bane of the mighty cockroach. For this reason, studies show that cockroaches use only latex paint in their homes.

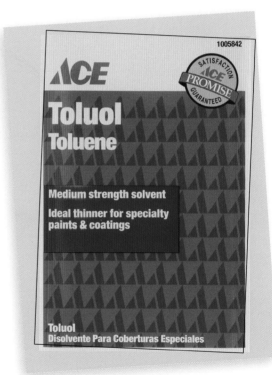

Acetone

Most commonly known as nail polish remover. Everyone knows the smell of Mom doing her nails, or, these days, Dad. Acetone is soluble in water, ether, ethanol and used in the manufacture of plastic fibers. It will remove super glue, and soften some epoxies and plastics. It is another solvent cleaner used in ink manufacturing. Our interest here is acetone as an additive to specific standard padding lacquers, and some aerosol spray finishes.

Toluene

Methylbenzene phenyl methane. No, it's not the eye doctor's vision chart — and that's about as technical you'll find here. Toluene occurs naturally in crude oil. It is another hydrocarbon petroleum distillate solvent with a sweet smell and is produced primarily in the making of gasoline. It will dissolve some paints and also acts as a thinning agent. It is used in many adhesives and lacquers and also in the manufacture of polyurethane foam.

Denatured alcohol

This is the solvent used for thinning shellac. This form of alcohol, or ethylated spirits, is ethanol rendered undrinkable — that is — toxic by the addition of additives (get a load of this: methanol, isopropanol, methyl ethyl keytone, methyl isobutyl keytone and denatonium, hence the *denatured* aspect of this particular solvent.) It is also used as fuel for alcohol lamps, and is a good solvent to use to wipe down sanded wood because alcohol will not raise the grain.

alcohol stove fuel
Methyl Hydrate 99.9% pure
combustible pour poêles à alcool
Hydrate de méthyle 99,9 % p

IDEAL FOR: Thinning shellac, cleaning shellac from brushes, cleaning windows, fondue fuel and fuel for marine unpressurized alcohol stoves.
IDÉAL POUR : diluer la gomme laque, nettoyer les pinceaux utilisés avec gomme laque, nettoyer les fenêtres, comme combustible à fondue et pour les poêles à alcool non pressurisé sur les bateaux.

CONTENTS MAY CATCH FIRE. CONTENTS HARMFUL. Do not smoke. Do n swallow. May cause blindness if swallowed. Use only in a well-ventilat area. Keep away from flames, such as a pilot light, and any object th sparks, such as an electric motor. Keep out of reach of children. To ope hold tab against cap and turn counter clockwise. To close - turn cap clo wise until tight.
FIRST AID TREATMENT: Contains methanol. If swallowed, call a Poison Control Centre or do immediately. If person is alert, do not induce vomiting.
LE CONTENU PEUT S'ENFLAMMER. CONTENU NOCIF. Ne pas fumer. Ne p avaler. L'ingestion peut causer la cécité. N'utiliser que dans un endroit b aéré. Tenir loin des flammes, telle une flamme pilote, et de tout objet prod sant des étincelles, tel un moteur électrique. Tenir hors de la portée d enfants. Pour ouvrir, tenir la languette contre la capsule et tourner dans sens antihoraire. Pour fermer, tourner la capsule dans le sens horaire et b serrer.
PREMIERS SOINS : Contient du méthanol. En cas d'ingestion, appeler immédiatement un c antipoison ou un médecin. Si la personne est consciente, ne pas provoquer le vomissement.

S-L-X
Denatured
Alcohol
Thins shellac. Cleans glass and metal.
Clean-burning fuel for marine stoves.
Alcohol Desnaturalizado

VM&P Naphtha

This solvent is made from liquid mixtures of hydrocarbons also distilled from petroleum. The initials VM&P stand for "Varnish Makers and Painter's". Naphtha is used mainly as a degreaser, oil-painting medium and for thinning paints and varnishes. Naphtha is also used in making shoe polishes, as well as an ingredient in some lighter fluids. A bit of naphtha added to oil paint will speed up drying time. Once again, here we see on the label the instructions to not swallow.

VM&P
Naphtha
A fast drying thinner for oil-based paint, enamel and varnish.
Nafta VM&P

DANGER! FLAMMABLE. KEEP AWAY FROM HEAT, SPARKS, FLAME AND ALL OTHER SOURCES OF IGNITION. VAPORS MAY CAUSE FLASH FIRE OR IGNITE EXPLOSIVELY. VAPORS MAY TRAVEL LONG DISTANCES TO OTHER AREAS AND ROOMS AWAY FROM WORK SITE. Do not smoke. Extinguish all flames and pilot lights, and turn off all stoves, heaters, electric motors and all other sources of ignition during use and until all vapors are gone. **USE ONLY WITH ADEQUATE VENTILATION TO PREVENT BUILDUP OF VAPORS.** Do not use in areas where vapors can accumulate and concentrate such as basements, bathrooms and small, enclosed areas. Whenever possible use outdoors in an open air area. If using indoors open all windows and doors and maintain a cross ventilation of moving fresh air across the work area. If strong odor is noticed or you experience slight dizziness – **STOP** – ventilation is inadequate. Leave area immediately. **IF THE WORK AREA IS NOT WELL VENTILATED, DO NOT USE THIS PRODUCT.** A dust mask does not provide protection against vapors.
DANGER! HARMFUL OR FATAL IF SWALLOWED. VAPOR HARMFUL. Contains Petroleum Distillates. Reports have associated repeated and prolonged overexposure to solvents with neurological and other physiological damage. Intentional misuse of this product by deliberately concentrating and inhaling vapors can be harmful or fatal. Avoid breathing of vapors or mist and contact with skin, eyes and clothing. Do not take internally.

CONTENTS MAY CATCH FIRE. CONTENTS HARMFUL. FUMES HARMFUL. Do not smoke. Do not swallow. May cause blindness if swallowed. Do not get in eyes or on skin or clothing. Keep out of reach of children. Use only in a well-ventilated area. Keep away from flames, such as a pilot light, and any object that sparks such as an electric motor. The spread of vapours from this material is very rapid. Wear rubber gloves.

To open - push cap down and turn counter clockwise. To close - push cap down and turn clockwise until tight.

FIRST AID TREATMENT: Contains toluene, methyl ethyl ketone, methanol and acetone. If swallowed, call a Poison Control Centre or doctor immediately. If person is alert, do not induce vomiting, as product can be aspirated into the lungs. If in eyes or on skin, rinse well with water. If on clothes, remove clothes.

LE CONTENU PEUT S'ENFLAMMER. CONTENU NOCIF. ÉMANATIONS NOCIVES. Ne pas fumer. Ne pas avaler. L'ingestion peut causer la cécité. Éviter tout contact avec les yeux, la peau et les vêtements. Tenir hors de la portée des enfants. N'utilise que dans un endroit bien aéré. Tenir loin des flammes, telle une flamme pilote, et d'un objet produisant des étincelles, tel un moteur électrique. La propagation de

Lacquer Thinner

Lacquer thinners are produced in varying grades depending on the combinations of solvents used in their manufacture, which is to say there are better quality lacquer thinners and lesser quality varieties. If you were spraying lacquer you would have to use a higher quality of thinner.

But this is not a book that concerns spraying in the home.

Once again, we see the label clearly instructs: Do not swallow.

Very important that this sinks in.

Lacquer thinner is used to dissolve, dilute or clean up lacquer products — including brushes. So don't use nylon or foam brushes with lacquer thinner or you'll be left holding the handle. (See page 79, The dissolving foam brush.)

Lacquer thinner will also remove marks on metal and dissolve adhesive residue. It will also remove unwanted guests if you open a can while they are in your house.

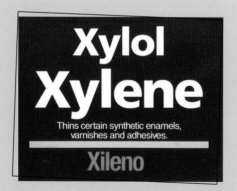

Klean-Strip® Xylene can be used in place of Toluene to thin specified oil-based paint, lacquer and varnish when a slower rate of evaporation is desired. Xylene will also remove certain adhesives, and is an excellent clean-up solvent for tools and equipment immediately after use.

DIRECTIONS FOR USE: Follow the coating manufacturer's instructions for the proper amount of Xylene required; do not use more than recommended.

IMPORTANT: Carefully read all directions, notes and cautions prior to use. Only use this product as directed on the label. Do not use as a fuel. Do not use for any other purpose. Do not mix with any other product. Do not spread this product over large surface areas because fire and health safety risks will increase dramatically. Protect eyes with chemical splash goggles and avoid prolonged skin contact.

HELPFUL TIPS: Use only as specified by the coating, adhesive or hobby product manufacturer. Do not use as a general purpose cleaner. Xylene may soften or damage plastics, synthetics and many other finishes. Use only where specified, and test an inconspicuous area before application. Do not use on linoleum, plastic, rubber, asphalt tile, fiberglass or other synthetic materials. **Xylene may harm these surfaces.**

Xylene

This is another solvent produced from petroleum. Sweet smelling like toluene, it is very flammable. Xylene is a solvent and thinner for some heavy-duty industrial paints and synthetic resin varnishes and is also used as a cleaning agent for silicon chips as well as industrial steel. Xylene will dissolve water-based finishes quite rapidly (see "Talk and no one listens," page 69) but would have had little or no effect whatsoever on my ex mother-in-law's cooking — except to perhaps have made it tastier.

The stains, paints and colors

Penetrating oil-based stains

On the shelves of hardware stores and home centers you will find oil stains in abundance as well as water-based stains. First, let's deal with the most common of these: oil stains.

Penetrating oil stains are by far the easiest kinds of stains for the amateur to get his or her hands on. They are inexpensive, come in a variety of colors and are intermixable. The major drawback with these types of stains is that they need to be applied in proper temperatures. Apply these below 50° and you will run into problems with drying and over 80° (especially if there's high humidity), you will run into the problem of the stain "sweating." (See chapter 3, Don't fret the sweat, page 62.)

All in all, I would say that penetrating oil stains are what the novice should begin working with.

Gel stains

Gel stains are another type of stain that come thickened so as to reduce splatter. Many people like using these types of stains because they just wipe on and wipe off. You can also purchase gel varnishes that rub on just the same.

POURING SOLVENTS

Take care when transferring solvents from one container to another. If you pour with the opening of the can down, air can't easily enter the container to replace the liquid and it forces its way in and causes splashing and a big mess. Pour with the opening on top and the air will happily enter the can and no mess occurs.

Water-based stains

Most oil paint may be reduced to a stain by thinning with mineral spirits or turpentine. When we think of latex paint we must remember that it may be thinned by using plain ordinary water or, if you wanted to get really fussy — distilled water — in order to dilute it to stain consistency. In essence then, this is what water-based stain is.

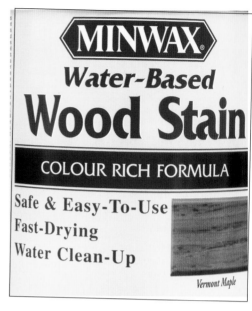

Many companies manufacture their own brands along with their oil-based varieties of stain, and, while oil-based varieties of stain contain VOCs (volatile organic compounds), water-based stains have none. Better for the environment, better for you.

The biggest disadvantage of water-based stains is that, because they are water based, they will raise the grain of the wood. So, in order the counteract the problem, you must first wet the wood lightly with a sufficiently damp sponge, allow the wood to dry and then cut the raised fibers by sanding be-fore you even get started staining. (See sidebar, Preparation for water-based finishes, page 67.)

Do you have to do this step? Let's just say it would be a wise thing to do.

The bottom line is, like everything else mentioned in these pages, water-based stains are there to be investigated. So grab your deerstalker cap and find your magnifying glass, Sherlock.

Aniline dyes

Aniline dyes are not readily available to the public.

That means you.

Aniline dyes must be ordered over the Internet from wood-working supply houses or other finishing supply sources. The furniture industry relies heavily on these types of dyes — the water-soluble type being the preferred favorite amongst professionals. However, when mixed, aniline dyes are 90% water-based, so you must remember, they too will raise the grain of the wood.

To make a quart, you usually mix a tablespoon or two of dye powder or crystals, $1/4$ cup or so of methanol and then $3 3/4$ cups of water.

Aniline dyes come in an amazing variety of colors and un-like penetrating oil stains, aniline dyes will really soak into and color the fibers of the wood — and your flesh!

You definitely have to wear gloves with this stuff.

I once got my hands into some green aniline dye and wound up substituting for the Jolly Green Giant in his niblet-corn commercial close-ups of the late 1970s! And don't get me started on what a pest his little buddy Sprout was.

Paints

The sure-fire coating for wood has always been paint. These days, paint comes in all colors and brand names. Home centers and fashion designers — even lady TV hosts — seem to have their fingers in the cans with their own line of colors available to the public. In fact, soon to be ex-Vice President Cheney is said to be coming out with what he calls his WMD (weapons of mass destruction) line of paints. Although, rumor has it, these will be hard to find.

So what is paint already?

Paint is varnish with pigment added. How simple is this to understand? Reduce the amount of pigment, take away the varnish, add some thinner, driers and presto! A stain is born.

Any paint, whether oil or latex, may be thinned to make a stain. I prefer oil paint but this is your own choice. Through experimentation you can decide which works best for you.

Many people have asked me about their kitchen cabinets over the years. Can we paint over the finish? We want to brighten the room. Is painting better than stripping and refinishing? And I would always say the same thing — do whatever you like. I'm not the one who's going to be doing the work, so, if you want to undertake the job of stripping and refinishing your kitchen cabinets, go right ahead. However, if you want to brighten a kitchen and save yourself some time — especially if the cabinets are not made of any special kind of wood — then paint is a sure thing.

I remember painting the kitchen cabinets in a house I once owned. These cabinets were Mylar faced, which is to say, they were made of pressboard that was covered in a wood-grained plasticky-like product not unlike contact paper.

I simply cleaned the surfaces with paint thinner, removed all the doors and hardware, sanded with 100-grit sandpaper, primed with an oil-based primer, (two coats, sanded between coats) and then applied two coats of semi-gloss enamel. The room went from dark drab walnut simulation to a semi-glossy vibrant blue in no time. The room looked bigger and brighter — even at night when the room usually gave the appearance of a cave.

JOE KNOWS...

That most wood fillers will not stain well, which is to say they will always absorb more stain than the wood. To counteract this problem, apply shellac to the dried putty before staining.

MAKE YOUR OWN

If you want to make your own wax sticks all you need is some beeswax, dry pigment and lemon oil. You need to melt the wax, so you will need some type of double boiler. A simple tin can and an old saucepan will do nicely. The procedure is as follows: Shave the wax and place it into the can. Add an inch or so of water to the saucepan and stick the can of shaved wax into the water. As the water boils, the heat will liquefy the wax. When the wax has liquefied, add your dry pigment and 5 or 6 drops of lemon oil (or mineral oil) per ounce. The oil will make the dried sticks more pliable. Roll some ordinary wax paper around a ³/₄" piece of dowel stick to make a tube, fold up one end, tape it closed and place a funnel in the open end. Pour the liquefied, colored wax into the tube through the funnel and leave the filled tube standing to cool and harden.

Wood fillers

Wood filler is usually over-used, as in the case of trying to repair the corner of a piece of furniture or a cabinet that's been damaged when a real wood patch would serve better. Believe me, I've seen it. There are many types of wood fillers on the shelves, exterior as well as interior. Make sure you use the right one when wood filler is necessary — you want to be sure to never use interior putty for outdoor work. Naturally, exterior putty used outdoors is just fine.

Wood glue

As with wood fillers, carpenter's wood glue comes in exterior and interior and the same rule applies: Do not use interior glue outside, but exterior glue may be used inside. And, if you like to work sloppy, wood glue can pose a real problem for the Oscar Madison-type woodworker. (See Chapter 2: Because of Glue, page 38.)

Putty pencils

These sticks are made from combinations of wax, oil and dry pigment and are the easiest to work with when filling minor scratches and nail holes.

Touch-up markers

Touch-up markers come in a variety of colors. The markers are used mainly for covering minor surface scratches or worn edges on finished surfaces. Choose the color that best suits your need. And don't lose the caps. If left lying around without their caps, markers will dry out.

The Finishes

Oil-based finishes

Oil-based finishes are as varied as my many aches and pains — and that's saying something! From paint to stains to protective clear coatings, oil-based products are a legion to say the least.

Since it's inception, the industry has been hastening to improve the "bubble bubble, toil and trouble" that was inherent in using the first wood finishes. They are creating newer tougher coatings for most applications. Originally, natural resins were dissolved in alcohol to create "spirit varnishes."

Today, synthetic resins are combined with oils and heated under pressure. Then, driers and thinners are added to speed the varnishes' drying time once it has been brushed on. Varnishes are made from resins such as alkyd or phenolic and then mixed with unsaturated oils such as soya, linseed or tung, to create varieties of coatings. Alkyd soya varnishes are furniture-grade varnishes. They are flexible, easy to work with and can be easily rubbed out.

Phenolic varnishes, or spar marine varnishes, are ideal for outdoor furniture, decks, boats, outdoor signs and just about anything else that sits out there. My aunt even used some on my uncle.

Spar varnish is sometimes referred to as "marine varnish," not because it was Gomer Pyle's favorite varnish, but for the flexibility of the dried film out of doors. Spars contain special plasticizers as well as additional UV (ultraviolet) blockers that help retard the breakdown of the dried film. Which means that our friendly sun will not cause them to deteriorate too quickly. These plasticizers work well on wood. As you may or may not know, wood continues to expand and contract with the changing seasons. In the summer for instance, all wood — varnished, painted or raw — will swell with humidity while in the winter wood will contract, or "shrink," — like my sanity.

For this reason, spars are ideal for outdoor use because the film dries slowly, due to the amount of oil in the mix. It is also for this reason that you do not want to use spar varnish for your interior furniture. It is much too soft. You need to know this, because if you walk into a paint store or home center and ask for a varnish, the sales person will, more often than not, give you spar varnish because they don't know how to use it.

Polyurethane

Believe it or not, polyurethane was discovered in 1848 by a German named Wurtz. He discovered isocyanate, one of the building blocks of polyurethane. During the 1930s polyurethane was developed for military use in Germany by Otto Bayer, who was also the first to make it commercially available — okay, when the bell rings go to hygiene class!

Polyurethanes are more closely related to Plexiglass and Lucite than resin varnishes. Polyurethanes are strong, long-lasting and durable, however they do have their drawbacks:

1. They cannot be polished up (rubbed out) as easily as varnish or lacquer.

2. Polyurethane needs to be re-coated exactly as the can instructs — the window of opportunity is critical — otherwise the second coat will not bond to the first.

3. Polyurethane cannot be re-coated years later as can varnish. The old finish must be stripped off completely before recoating can take place. In other words, you must start from scratch.

That said, I do like polyurethane for its quickness in drying and there's no reason why you couldn't incorporate polyurethane and varnish on a piece of furniture, such as a desk, where the frame could be brushed with polyurethane and the top could be finished with a more repairable (able to be rubbed out) varnish.

CONTAINS MINERAL SPIRITS

Inspecting the label of a can will tell you, first and foremost, not to swallow the contents, and then: Contains mineral spirits. This informs you right off the bat that the product is **not** water washable. You should never smoke when using oil-based products (or *any* solvent-based product), get it in your eyes or breathe solvent vapors.

Other key words that allow you to identify oil-based products would be: Turpentine, naphtha, toluene and/or xylene.

CONTENTS MAY BE HARMFUL. MAY IRRITATE EYES. MAY IRRITATE SKIN. Do not swallow. Do not get in eyes, or on skin or clothing. Do not breathe fumes. Keep out of reach of children. Keep away from flames or sparks. Wear rubber gloves, and safety glasses. Use only in a well-ventilated area. **FIRST AID TREATMENT:** Contains Mineral Spirits. If swallowed, call Poison Control Centre or a doctor immediately. Do

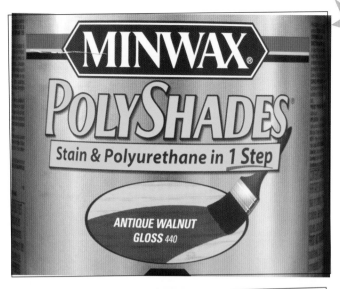

Poly-stains

These finishing products are sold under different names, such as Polyshades, but they are simply polyurethanes that have a stain incorporated into the mix. These purport to save you a step because you are applying a stain and a protective topcoat in one step, so you will have that much more time to move the house to the left like the wife's been wanting you to do.

Surprise: They don't work as well as you might think. As a single application material on new wood they are questionable. Applied over a previously stained surface the look can be enhanced. (See photo 7, page 87.)

Think of polyshades as akin to washing your head with a shampoo/conditioner in one bottle. Are you really that much in a hurry that you can't first, shampoo, rinse and then condition? Besides, most hair authorities say 2-in-1 formulas are not as good at doing one and then the other. I am telling you that staining your wood first, allowing it to dry fully and then applying a Polyshade for added depth of color and luster is much better than a 2-in-1 step anything.

Varathane

Varathane is a brand name. The finish is a variant of a petroleum-based urethane that stands up well under traffic. It is good for furniture as well as floors and can be thinned up to 15% to increase the time you have to work with it. Its main ingredient is aliphatic naphtha, so it is fairly quick drying.

Lacquers

Without going into a bunch of specifics on the structure, kinds, etc. of lacquer, suffice it to say lacquer is highly volatile and the fumes can be overpowering, so it is best to use this finishing material in a well-ventilated room.

Most industry lacquer finishes are sprayed on and can be either clear or pigmented. If the homeowner does not have the ability to spray, brushing lacquers are available in high-gloss, semi-gloss or satin sheens. Brushing lacquers will usually set up in thirty minutes and be ready for recoating (depending on weather conditions) in about an hour.

Lacquer is a solvent-release finish, which means the solvent evaporates and what's left behind is a dry film. When you apply a second coat of lacquer, that second coat is going to eat into the first one and create one thicker coat.

Oils well

As a finishing material, boiled linseed oil has some history.

I have met many people over the years that have told me too many tales of grandmother recipes that have been handed down through the ages. These recipes for oiling wood may contain lemon, vinegar, wine — even urine. Minus the last ingredient, I think you'll agree that it sounds more like what's been handed down is salad dressing rather than a finish for wood. The method is always the same though. Using a brush, apply linseed oil to the raw, sanded, wood — saturate the heck out of it. Let it sit to soak in for a couple of days then wipe the surfaces down and then let sit for two weeks. Next (now get ready for this, so help me it's true!), rub more oil into the wood once a week — for six months!

Six months!

If you have a life, disregard these instructions, but I have known people who have accomplished this and are still oiling something that had been handed down to them — the flesh of hands worn to transparent, oily representatives of things that could have once been called blood-filled flesh.

The problem with linseed oil is that it never really dries, and the smell, unless you like the smell (which I do), can be overpowering. Oiled surfaces will also collect dirt, dust and grime over the years, but some treasure this look. If you don't mind wiping a lot, give it a try. It's for you to decide. Oil finishes will repel water quite well. (See photo 6, page 87.) Just be sure to discard any oil-soaked rags in a bucket of water. Always have a bucket handy while you work because linseed oil, given the right conditions, has been known to spontaneously ignite. Years ago in Philadelphia a major fire took place right in the center of the city on the fifteenth floor of the Meridian Building where some knucklehead finishers, who were oiling wainscotting, left their oil-soaked rags in a closet with their other cleaning materials.

The rags happened to be near a heating source and, well, marshmallows anyone?

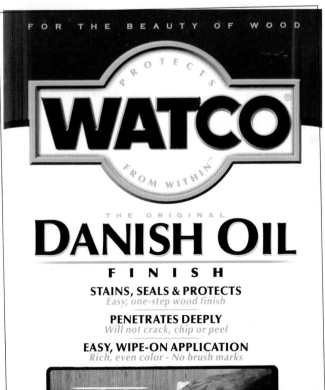

Wood conditioners

Many manufacturers of wood finishing products produce what are called conditioners. These products are usually oil-based. A conditioner (another name would be sealer, which is what they used to be called) is used specifically for woods that stain unevenly or become blotchy once a stain enters the wood. Finishes on woods such as pine, birch and cherry benefit greatly from the application of a conditioner because these woods often absorb more stain in places where the sap wood may run heavy, causing uneven appearances or splotching.

Sanding sealers predate wood conditioners

Back in the 1980s, there were oil-based mixtures of thinners, drying agents and oils that companies manufactured to work with their various oil stains. However, because they are both petroleum-based products, the disadvantage is they cancel each other out. Let me explain.

I was called in on a job at the last minute on a million dollar home being built in Philadelphia. My friend was the general contractor/project manager on that job and he didn't feel it necessary to call me until he ran into a problem. Of course there's always a problem.

The job was nearing completion, he was going crazy, the rug people were coming in three days, every detail was taken care of except for the finishing of all the new wood — you see where I'm going with this?

This is why it's called finishing, folks! Not only is it the last thing that's done, as far as general contractors are concerned, it's the last thing they ever think about.

So, the problem was created by my friend's boss, who, in an effort to save a few bucks, decided to have his daughters, ages 13 and 15, apply product to all doors, baseboards and window sills throughout the house. No foolin'. What's more, they were applying said sanding sealer to wood that had been colored with an oil-based, red mahogany stain.

The effect it was causing is what prompted my friend to finally relent and call me. Seems that as the girls went about slapping on the sanding sealer, a funny thing seemed to be taking place — their cans of clear liquid began turning red as the brushed sanding sealer re-dissolved the not yet dried oil stain they had applied to the wood! The surface was streaking, uneven and blotchy. What to do? What to do?

Once I got on the job I was finished in two days. First, with lacquer thinner, I cleaned everything off the wood they had already messed up; a job in itself. I then re-stained to the desired color, and, instead of using sanding sealer, I used thinned shellac. Because it is alcohol based, it will seal an oil stain without pulling it from the surface of the wood.

Once the shellac had dried, it was only a matter of lightly sanding all wood surfaces, applying my clear finish, and collecting a check.

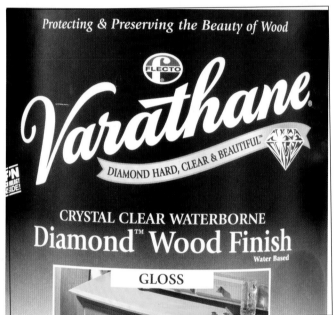

Acrylic polyurethane (water cleanup)

Water-based polyurethanes are all over the place. They are hard, tough and made up of acrylic polyurethane dispersed in water along with glycol ethers. Each manufacturer has a different formula, but essentially, they all clean up with water.

They don't smell as bad as their solvent-based kin and they are resistant to scuffing. However, the finish is quite flat, especially if you've stained your wood (with a water-based stain) a dark mahogany or walnut. The effect is a dull, washed and lifeless look — kind of like Paris Hilton's first-day wake-up in the cell or the current Britney picture in the supermarket tabloid of your choice.

Shellac finishes

Shellac has been around a long time — longer even than Larry King — who was once court jester to Nebuchadnezzar.

Shellac is the only natural finish on the market. Orange shellac comes that way from the refining process and it's great for rendering a warm antique look, especially on wood that has been stained brown. White shellac, now called clear, (even though it's more of a dirty white color due to the bleaching process it undergoes to get rid of the orange tone), is best for those finishes where an amber luster is not necessary.

Shellac comes from the laccifer lacca insect, or, parasite that enjoys meals of sap from Banyan trees in India. Shellac can be purchased in dry-flake form or liquid.

Shellac was the major finishing material used throughout time up to about 1850. It may perhaps be best represented through the French polishing technique. French polishing was the standard finish used throughout the world. It's a finish that is applied with a linen rag containing a wool core that has been soaked in shellac. (See pages 100-103.)

You know, before sanding sealers and wood conditioners, the one true sealer that was available was good old shellac. You could walk into a store and buy orange or white shellac. No problem. Then, all of a sudden, there was a time in the late 1980s when it became increasingly hard to find. I would always get, "They don't use that much anymore," from the hardware store gents. And I would be saying to them, and myself: "I use it! There's gotta be other people out there who use it too!" Then, when I was on television at the beginning of the 1990s, (and I know I have no real proof of this) all of a sudden it was out there again all over the shelves! Shellac was all over the place, albeit with a changed "under-label" name.

It was now called Shellac, sealer-undercoater.

Orange was now amber and white shellac was labeled as being clear.

Could this have anything to do with my always saying, show after show: "applying a wash-coat of orange shellac over your stained piece of furniture will give it a nice amber glow?"

And you know I still wonder.

But to be honest, I can't attribute this change solely to myself. I mean, I know it was not only me who brought it into vogue — but after all — I did do over 152 television shows and I would say that more than two-thirds of those shows involved shellac. This, combined with various companies coming out with what they called sanding sealers, the kind of which I touched upon earlier — the kind that the bosses' daughters were using on the woodwork that I wound up fixing — in conjunction with the word sealer having become so firmly etched in the mind of the weary consumer, just may have convinced the shellac companies to change the wording on their cans.

Of course, people such as myself have always known of shellac's true brilliance.

Shellac may be used as a sealer if you are going to use an oil-based stain on your wood, but should not be used if you are going to use water-based stains, varnishes or polyurethanes.

Shellac is the beginners' finish and the most basic ingredient to all finishing. Shellac is great for everything save for tabletops and outdoor wood. It remains my favorite finish because of its dynamic nature.

As a novice you should know, regardless of what the label of the can will say about not using shellac as a sealer, that shellac has been and always may be used as a sealer for oil stains or as a sealer for raw wood before applying your varnish topcoat. You may also use shellac as a sealer/undercoat for lacquer finishes, but never use shellac under polyurethane.

The other stuff you'll need

Sandpaper

Utilizing my card-shark skills, you see me here as I fan a deck of sandpapers from 80-grit up to 600-grit wet/dry. The type of paper you use is very important to the job you are about to undertake. (See sanding chart page 41.)

Sanding blocks

Sanding blocks ranging in grits from 80 to 100 are good for mouldings and they come in their own slipcase! When these clog, you can clear their surfaces by scrubbing a brass brush over them. The same applies to regular sandpaper.

Abrasive pads

Abrasive pads are the new kids on the block. They are good for cleaning old finish from surfaces when stripping (and they won't give you those nasty steel wool slivers that are not at all fun). They cannot be used as the abrasive of choice for roughing up the surface between coats of clear finish, or, for rubbing out any type of clear finish for that satiny smooth look.

Steel wool

Steel wool, like sandpaper, comes in many different grades. On the left is coarse No.0 — resembling steel shredded wheat. This type of steel wool is good for removing old and flaking paint in conjunction with paste removers. On the right I'm holding No.0000 steel wool, the finest and softest — like steel cashmere — which is always used for rubbing out and polishing finishes.

Dust masks

Whenever you set out to sand or use steel wool, you should always wear a dust mask. I know the impulse for most is to by the cheapest, but really folks, you should splurge when it comes to dust masks — and buy the double-banded type so they fit tightly against your face and prevent dust from being inhaled from around the edges.

Gloves

Disposable or not disposable gloves? Whichever you like. For simple staining, vinyl or latex work well. A box of a 100 vinyl gloves is the type I prefer. These cost about $8.

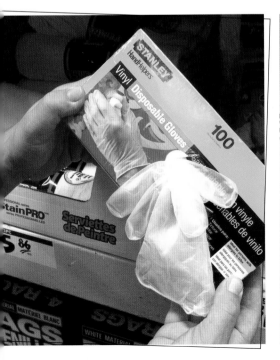

Paint strainers

I use these for straining shellac, especially when I make my own using dry flakes. (See page 73.) Strainers work well for just about any type of paint or varnish, especially those that may have bits of dried stuff in them, which occurs when the lid hasn't been put back on right.

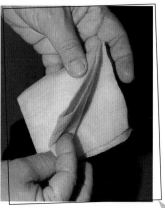

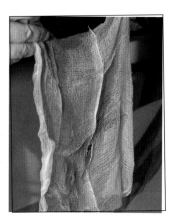

Tack cloth

Tack cloths are great for picking up final traces of sanding dust, but exactly what they are made of is anybody's guess. I know its cheesecloth with the cheese removed. Kidding. They actually are cheesecloth that has been impregnated (so someone wrote me when I'd questioned it on TV years ago) with neoprene. Neoprene, just so you know, is a type of rubber. Makes sense, eh?

The mistake that most people make with these things is that they never open them up. And by opening up I do not mean neatly and squarely so that it fits back into the plastic wrapper. I mean pulling it apart until it becomes a fluffy mass (like a ball) to wipe surfaces. The idea is to separate the layers. The more you use it and fold it in on itself is how it stays sticky, because the sticky coating will continue to eat the dust. If you keep one of these babies in a jar with a lid, (if you're into saving things) it will stay soft and sticky for a long, long time.

Wire brushes

From the picture, you can see that wire brushes also come in many varieties. They can be as small as toothbrushes and as big as scrub brushes. They are mostly identifiable when used for removing flaking paint from iron gates or metal patio furniture. However, for the wood finisher in the know, these babies are invaluable (see page 49), not only in the stripping process but also for cleaning the pores of oak and ash when pertinent to the desired effect. (See page 104.)

The brushes and applicators

Brushes are many and many are cheap. But you know cheap has its grades as do the good variety. For instance, these fanned out brushes are a typical array of "throw away" brushes. This means you can use them and clean them in the appropriate solvent, or, you can toss them when you've finished with them. The two black ones are Chinese bristle, the rest are hog hair. On the left is a four incher that I usually use for larger surfaces. I have used these with great success when applying lacquer, shellac, varnish and paint. They are also good for basting your favorite ribs with barbecue sauce. Just be sure to use a clean one, eh?

At the bottom of the brush scale we have the foam variety of brush, which can only be used with latex and some oil products. To play it safe, I would stick to water-based stuff with these guys. (See page 79.) The handles are real wood too, so before you toss them, saw off the handles. They can be used for plugs, dowels or you can make your own Lincoln Logs!

Two brushes hugging but, just like people, they're different. The one on the left is a natural-hair brush and can be used for oil paints as well as shellac. The one on the right is a nylon bristle brush for latex and water-based coatings. (Don't dare use nylon bristles for oil paint or lacquer.)

Here are a variety of brushes from my box. You can tell how much they've been used by the dried paint on the handles. At the top is a badger fitch brush, good for shellac, followed by some Robert Simmons flat artists brushes (see The Art Supply Store, page 74) and a couple of brand new $1/2$" rounds that I hadn't had time to dirty up before we took the pictures.

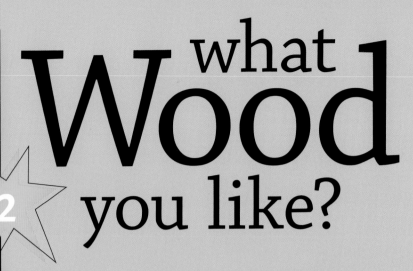

what Wood you like?

2

Ahh — there's the rub — er, I mean iron. In this chapter I want to lead you along the path of righteousness and of what to do and what not to do in the area of wood preparation. You know your finish job is only as good as the prep time you put into the finished product, so pay attention. There's going to be a quiz at the end of the book.

Woods the amateur woodworker likes to use

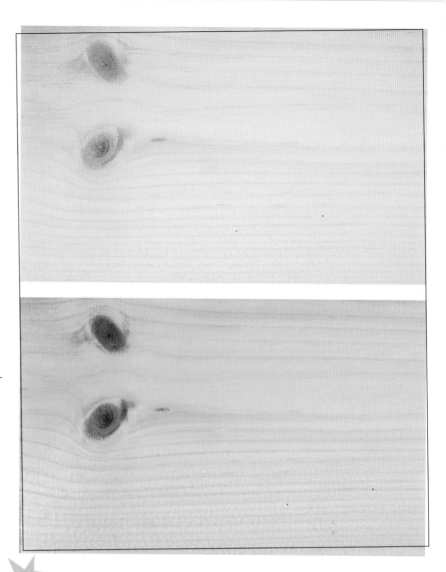

For certain, another bane of the novice finisher is sanding what you've built. From the outset you have to know when to sand and what to sand with. In other words, I'm talking "wood-prep."

Careful attention to the wood's surface before staining and top-coating with any of the available products you will find on the shelf is important. Unless, of course, you're looking for that rustic look then all you need is a hammer or an army of kids with Tonka trucks.

And, in order to pay attention to the surface you have to know (or should know, especially if you're the one who built it) what wood you are working with. Here's a list of seventeen wood types: **Oak, ash, walnut, chestnut, elm, butternut, birch, beech, gum, maple, cherry, mahogany, poplar, pine, redwood, cedar and spruce**.

I think of these seventeen, maybe about eight are familiar upon sight. Oak for tables, walnut banister, birch kitchen cabinets, maple butcher block, a pine bookcase, and, perhaps, a redwood deck or picnic table.

With the exception of my friend Albert, who buys many board feet of rough-hewn American black walnut and hoards it like a squirrel stores nuts, I think I would be right in assuming that most people may recognize six or seven of these woods and, that most woodworkers prefer to work with oak or pine first, mahogany and maple second, and then, perhaps, like my friend, Albert, walnut.

Let's take a look at these particular woods.

White pine

By and large, pine is the wood most used by the amateur. And, although pine is not really considered a furniture wood, there have been several styles of furniture made from pine over the years.

There are many species of pine but the ones most used would be white pine, knotty white pine, yellow pine and sugar pine. These woods are relatively soft, can be dented with a finger nail if pressed hard enough, and, as far as cutting with saws go, easy to work with. They are relatively smooth woods and never need fillers of any type. Much colonial furniture was constructed from pine and then painted. Pine sands well, but it is best not to sand with an orbital sander lest ye make them thar notorious squiggle marks (see page 46), which really don't show themselves until the stain is applied.

Plain sawn red oak   Quartersawn white oak   Rift cut red oak

Oak

Oak is probably the most common wood used for furniture and is the most versatile. There are over one hundred fifty species of oak, broken up into categories of white and red.

White oak is denser and a straw color. It's free of the pink tinge so evident in red oak — from whence it derives its name. To the untrained eye there may be no difference between the two woods, until you see them side by side.

You can clearly see a difference in these pictures.

You can do more things with oak than any other wood. Oak has been used for fine antiques and rustic furniture, as well as frames for sofas, pallets and down the line to casks for delicious red wines.

Depending on the cut of the wood, that is, the way the wood is halved and quartered into plain sawn, quartered or rift cut, the effects can be innumerable.

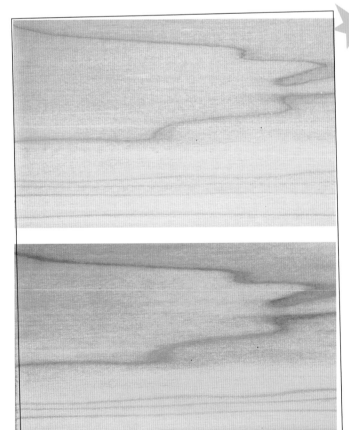

Poplar

Poplar is the everything wood and one of my favorite trees. My wife can smell a poplar three miles away — and that's nothing — she can smell a smoker in front of us in his car, a whole half mile up the road, on a blustery winter day with the windows closed and a head cold. But I digress.

I can't tell you the number of tables, chairs and benches that were brought to me over the years — when my shop was going strong — by people who thought they thought they were the bearers of some elegant treasure. And with one look I could tell them what they bore was poplar.

As for color, poplar can be made to look like other woods and is very often used in conjunction with walnut or mahogany. Poplar stains extremely well, and in the 1940s and 1950s, there was a period when absolutely everything made from poplar was being colored to resemble mahogany. In the furniture industry, this type of finish came to be called — and still is — a mahoganized finish.

Mahogany

Like oak, mahogany comes in many species. Because of its versatility, mahogany has been one of the woods favored by craftsman and fine furniture makers throughout history — Thomas Chippendale, Thomas Sheraton, Heppelwhite and Phyfe (that's Duncan Phyfe, not Barney!).

Of the three major types of mahogany, namely, Philippine, Luan and African, it is the African variety that is most highly favored and, indeed, more costly. It is the densest of the three and more finely figured, as well having a wonderful, deep natural red color.

The Luan and Philippine range from light pink to blondish yellow to an almost grey, blasé (kind of yech!) color. I spent a lot of my journeyman years sanding the heck out of mahogany shelves, tables, bar-tops, restaurant tabletops — even floors. I worked with Headley wood design and, as they always boasted, "It took us twice the time!" But what you got, I must say, was always beautiful.

Everything Headley did was made of mahogany that I would finish with their typical recipe of spar varnish, linseed oil and turpentine, which I rubbed on and buffed off.

Remember that mahogany may be purchased as veneer — and just because something is made with veneer doesn't make it cheap.

Walnut

Walnut has always been labeled "the man's wood," maybe because it's the classic wood used for gun stocks. You know, cowboys like John Wayne and all that. Walnut is a dense wood, ranging from a chocolatey brown to greyish-green color, with dark-colored streaks. Throughout the centuries, many pieces of historic furniture have been created from this wood. And, like mahogany, there are several types of walnut veneer available through woodworking supply companies.

The late George Nakashima, furniture maker extraordinaire, was quite fond of using walnut in a lot of his creations. I once visited his studio in New Hope, Pennsylvania and stood before a slab of European walnut that had been cut from a tree of enormous height — cut like a piece of ham. (The tree had been felled by lightning.) The ten-inch thick slice was irregularly beautiful and leaning against the studio wall — all twenty feet of it. It was waiting for its trip to Russia to be used as an altar.

The one thing that keeps amateurs away from using walnut is the price.

Cherry

Cherry is as beautiful as wood gets. There ain't a finer-aging wood than cherry. Its natural color ranges from dark reddish brown to a pale pink. The sapwood of cherry is usually white.

Cherry is used mainly for furniture, paneling, architectural woodwork and veneers. And let me say that furniture made from cherry can be quite costly too, so always be leery of so-called dinning sets — four-piece sets nonetheless — with six or eight dinning chairs for $899 or less.

No way, no time, no how, pal!

The sign probably says cherry finish, which is a lot different. This denotes that the set and accompanying chairs are made from birch, maple or both and then colored with stains and toning sprays to make it appear like cherry. Of course, the fact that maple and birch have similar grain markings makes the illusion even more complete.

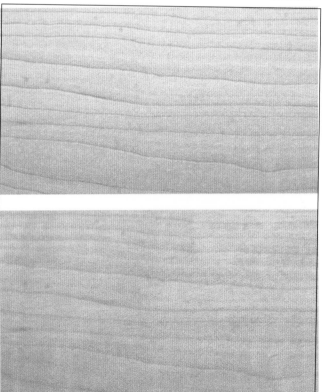

Yellow birch

Yellow birch is used for furniture, boxes, doors and veneered plywood. It's a durable, hard, tight-grained wood that, as far as I'm concerned, looks best when it's finished natural. Staining birch plywood is difficult only when you don't know how (see Chapter 3) and when you do, you can put solid and plywood together to render a copacetic effect.

Maple

If you have a butcher-block, you can count on it being maple. Kitchen cabinets can be made of maple; as well as handles, doors, spoons and chairs. I've finished floors made of maple but I don't cherish the look unless the finish is natural. Maple is another of those woods that can blotch when stain is applied. So, rather than trying to eradicate the blotching, I'll go with a natural finish.

Prep work for the wood

Because of glue

Glue is always a problem. Remember that I told you this when you are about to put finish on something you've spent a lot of time making.

Read on.

Although, I suppose I should say it's you, the "gluer," and not necessarily the glue that's the problem. Glue is in the bottle and quite harmless until it's squeezed from the bottle to join wood.

I once worked in of a shop where a particular bucket known as the "glue-bucket" — which wasn't filled with glue at all — hung from a large nail on the wall. This bucket hung empty until glue work began.

Then the bucket would be lifted from the nail and filled with water. The water would re-activate and soften the hard clump of sea sponge (which had been lying dormant in the dry bucket) which looked like something from a 1950's science fiction movie: black, tinges of blue-green, irregularly shaped, a non-beating, blackened alien — well, you get the point. This is what everyone used to wipe away any and all oozing glue.

Not a good idea.

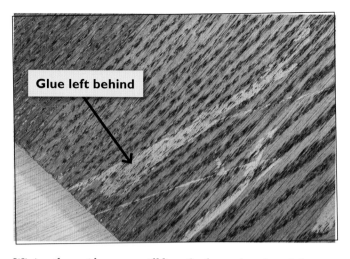

Wiping the residue away will liquefy glue and re-deposit it to the raw wood in thin smears. The wet wood will appear neat and ready for finish. But come time to stain and it will show up as clear, and, as sure as the invisible man's form, traceable in the rain.

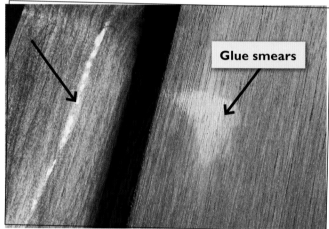

There are two schools of thought about getting rid of excess glue; wiping the glue away with a soaking wet sponge, wet rag or a finger, or by allowing the glue to set up for forty-five minutes or so and then simply peeling it away.

The later will save you grief — the former supplies it.

I don't for the life of me know why this simple fact isn't as plain as day but it's not, and so, the wiping away of glue with wet rags and sponges continues to be performed in woodworking circles everywhere.

I get many letters asking what to do in the case of smeared glue. Wood's been stained. Glue shows up. Oh wo is me!

Don't do it!

No matter how great the urge, no matter how drawn to rag and water you are (a divining rod bobbing to parched earth in search of H_2O), please, just hit yourself in the head with a hammer and say NO!

JUST WHAT IS OXALIC ACID?

Oxalic acid is bleach in crystal form that is mixed with hot water. It is at most an iffy bleach that may or may not work to remove black marks in wood. Wood bleached with Oxalic acid must be washed with water and vinegar to neutralize the bleaching action. Any sanding dust from wood that has been bleached with oxalic acid can irritate throat and nasal passages. It's usually easier to use straight Clorox.

Clamps and glue

No, this part is not about some insignificant comedy team from the 1940s. What I am referring to are the unsightly marks that can be created when wood is clamped up and a lot of glue has been used.

You will find as the glue oozes up and out it may sometimes gather round the clamp that's touching the wood. Left to dry in this way, not only will the glue harden around the clamp, but glue, you will find, has a particularly nasty habit of turning black overnight because the water content of the glue will react to the metal of the clamp.

As a safety measure, use some wax paper between the clamp and the wood.

Dried glue reacts with metal pipe.

Yuck! Results: Stain

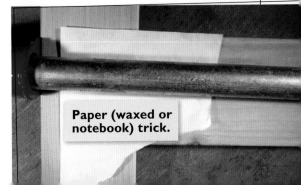

Paper (waxed or notebook) trick.

If you apply too much glue and then clamp, the glue will ooze from every inch of space under pressure of the clamp. If you apply too little glue, you won't have a proper bond. It's as simple as that.

SANDING CHART

Pine, Poplar, Mahogony:		Oak, Walnut, Cherry, Maple, Birch:	
80	rough work	60	removes planer marks
100	follow-up to rough work	80	follow-up sanding
220	final sanding	100	finish sanding

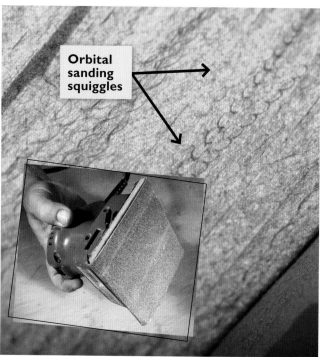

Orbital sanding squiggles

Time to prep

I do not mean this title as a call to arms, but rather to impress upon you the ethic of how important it is that you spend the time to do the prep work — and doing it the proper way. After all, (he said knowingly), if it's going to produce the proper results for you, why wouldn't you want to buckle down and spend some time getting to know the wood? It's not like you have to buy the wood a few drinks first.

All new wood is to be sanded.

What type of wood you're working with usually determines the type of paper you should use. And rather than run the gamut of sandpaper with lists and industry MOH scales (the industry scale which determines the hardness of the particular grit and or mineral structure, i.e. garnet, silicon-carbide, aluminium oxide) I will tell you to stick with 60-, 80-, 100- and 220-grit only — and higher grits only if you are doing specific oil finishes. (See Chapter 4.)

If you are using a belt sander (inset photo left) for preliminary work, that is, if the wood is rougher (photo at left) than the kind you are likely to find at the home center, where most of the wood purchased has been sanded to a presentable smoothness, I would stay with 80- and 100-grit sandpaper as well to kill the rough spots. You may then finish off with a pleasant hand sanding.

The same rule applies to orbital sanders (inset photo lower left). And I must say, that although I do not disapprove of any sanding device, I like to enforce the rule that no matter how high in grit you may rise to, hand sanding afterwards is going to eradicate squiggles (photo lower left).

See the Sanding Chart above. This is as simple a guide as can be provided for sanding the woods I've mentioned from rough to smooth. Keep in mind that most sandpaper is of the aluminium oxide or garnet varieties. Which is better? Years ago, a cabinetmaker's cabinet would have contained only garnet. Nowadays however, aluminium oxide has the slight edge because it will last longer, but either one is fine.

When sanding to higher grits, (especially if you are working with harder woods such as oak, maple, and birch) the higher you sand, and the more you sand to get that wood as satiny smooth as you think it ought to be, the less the oil-based wiping stain is going to be effective. Sanding to higher grits closes the pores of the wood; close the pores and your stain will not penetrate. If you are attempting an oil/wax finish or an oil/shellac/wax finish, (see Chapter 4), sand away to you heart's content or until your fingers are gone!

Wear-Throughs

When I was a kid, my father used to call my play pants my "knockarounds" — to differentiate them from my good, dress pants — the single pair of blue dress pants I owned.

Wear-throughs bears the same sort of cadence to my ears, and, I suppose you could say my knockarounds had more than their fair share of wear-throughs. I know it sounds crazy, but this is how my brain joins things together and, really, would you want me any other way?

But just what are wear-throughs?

Glad you asked.

First let me tell you another, teeny story — because I got a million of them — from the same shop where the glue bucket was so prominent. This shop was the proud employer of what I liked to refer to as The Dirty Dozen Crappy Sanders. And here's why.

Let's say they had made counters, or, a thirty-foot run of bar front comprised of solid and plywood, bound for some new, swank, center-city restaurant. No matter how big or small, I don't care what it was, the wood would always be poorly sanded — en masse, by orbital and air compressed random orbit sanders. The advance in sanding technology would not benefit this Dirty Dozen.

No such luck. And I was always the one who wound up having to touch up their mistakes, namely, their wear-throughs.

Just imagine if you can, five to ten guys armed with various sanders, checking the clock for break time, working through lunch with drippy, South Philadelphia sandwiches in one hand and their sanders buzzing away in the other, carelessly inattentive to their machine's abrading the wood, all the while complaining of having lost on the football pool the previous day.

They would make squiggles with the orbital sanders and wear through the veneer of expensive plywood. Their machines would round over counter edges that should have been hard, or, sharp arises (where one plane meets another). But worst of all, they consistently scarred any and all wood with eighth-inch deep arcs from the heads of their compressed-air orbiting disc sanders.

1 Once you have worn through the veneer of plywood to expose the underlayment, there is little you can do but try and hide the bare truth. The first thing to do is coat the area with a spit coat of shellac using a fine brush. Remember a spit coat means 1 part shellac from the can to 5 parts denatured alcohol or methyl hydrate. (See page 58.)

2 Spray some spray shellac directly onto the wax paper pallet, (and remember to spray the shellac onto the pallet first before you sprinkle any dry pigment — otherwise the force of air from the spray can will blow the dry pigment away. I don't know how many times I've done it without thinking.) The touch up colors needed for maple are French yellow ochre, white, a bit of raw umber and a smidge of vermilion.

3 With practice you can conceal anything. The next step after hiding a wear-through would be to apply the protective top-coat. As a rule, this type of cover-up works best on vertical areas, that is, sides, fronts, edges, but may be extremely difficult, if not impossible on a top surface.

Folding sandpaper thrice

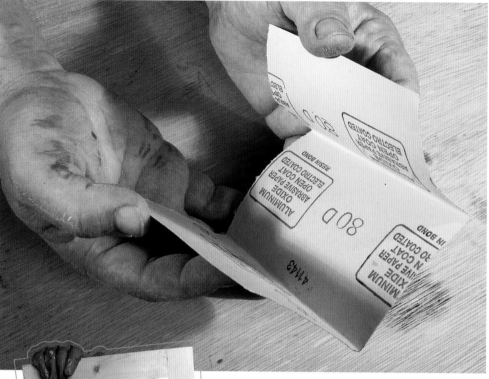

Sandpaper should be halved and then folded three times. It's not written in stone — or sand. Ha! But it's the way I've been doing it for most of my career.

2 Held this way, it shall not fail thee if thou shalt remember to pay attention to what thou art doing and not sanding just up to thy coffee break.

JOE KNOWS...

That sandpaper should be folded three times.

3 Sandpaper will always tell you when it's done and needs to be turned.

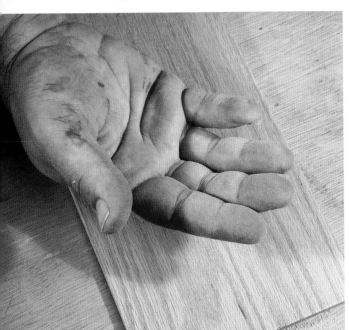

4 If you become aware of a feeling, which kind of resonates within your fingertips, you will be wasting your energy working with paper that doesn't have any cutting ability.

5 This is a halved sheet of 80-grit sandpaper that's been folded in thirds and turned six times.

More sanding tips

• Do not cross the grain, especially where, for instance, a rail meets a stile, because these kinds of nasty scratches will show up terribly once stain is applied.

• Placing a piece of masking tape over where a crossover scratching can occur and proceeding with caution can eliminate this type of common problem.

• Sand all wood evenly, and with equal pressure and with the same grit!

I kid you not. I have seen work where the person sanded a bureau with 80 grit and then went to 100 grit, forgetting to sand one side of said bureau with the 100-grit paper, so the 80-grit sanded side wound up appearing much darker than the other because the wood was that much more open to sucking up the stain.

Do not sand across the grain, for example; where a rail meets a stile. These kinds of scratches will look horrible when the stain is applied.

2 Place a piece of masking tape over the area where a crossover scratching can occur.

3 Proceed with caution when sanding.

★ Easing sharp edges

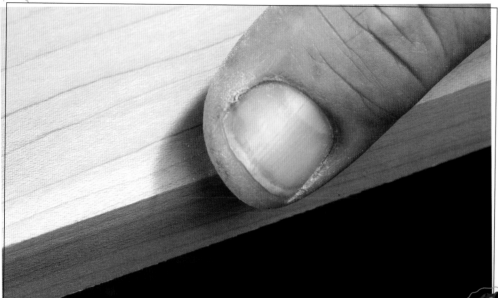

Be sure to ease (not obliterate) any sharp edges or, to get technical, arises — where one plane meets another.

OUCH!

Sharp edges can cut you!

JOE KNOWS...

That dampening the wood once you've finished sanding — and with sharp eyes — you will be able to determine if the squiggles are gone.

Out darn squiggles

I like to enforce the rule that no matter how high in grit you may rise to, hand sanding afterwards is going to eradicate squiggles left by machine sanding.

I reiterate what I've told you earlier only because I think it needs repeating so I'm going to insist on this being bold:

Any time you use a machine to sand, go over it with the next higher grit, and do it by hand — which is to say — if you use 80 grit on your orbital sander, the next step should be to hand sand using 100 grit to complete the job.

Edge treatments

Sometimes, out of necessity — or maybe you're just plain cheap — you need to cut corners. A lot of woodworkers will edge-band plywood or particleboard with iron-on wood veneers that come rolled in wheels resembling old-time reel-to-reel tape recording spools.

Or they do it the preferred way using solid stock to reinforce the strength of the plywood, which is especially important if you're making shelves on which you intend arranging heavy books. If plywood or particleboard shelves aren't reinforced with solid stock edge banding, they will gradually bend under weight.

I have been in many a situation where all I've had on hand was a piece of particleboard without tools or time — or both — but needed to get moving. Like the time I made a drawing board for a friend and, because it was a rush job (last-minute birthday gift), I had to use what was around the shop and simply filled the porous edges (always reminiscent of the ever-popular Rice Krispies treats.) with ordinary wood filler.

This is more of a design effect I agree, but one of those things you're better off knowing than not knowing. Any wood filler may be used here. Simply scoop a bit from the container with a utility knife blade and scrape it across the edge. The idea, of course, is to force the filler into the pores of the surface. Remove as much excess as possible with the edge of the blade.

When the filler has dried, sand with 100-grit paper. At this point, examine the edge to see if it's going to need a second application of wood filler. If so, apply again, allow the second application of filler to dry, and then sand — and sand again.

You can use any type of paint to color the filled edge. Here I am using ordinary posterboard, or Tempera paint (see chapter 3), which is water-soluble and will therefore dry quickly. Once the paint dries, apply a sealer coat of thinned shellac, allow it to dry, and then sand with 320-grit silicon carbide sandpaper. Paint a second coat of edge color, allow this to dry and sand with 320-grit silicon carbide paper. Paint a second coat of color.

Once the second coat of paint has dried, you can seal the band of color with a wash coat (thinned to about 1 part shellac to 3 parts alcohol) of shellac and then apply any type of clear finish over top. Here, I applied a couple of coats of satin spray lacquer over all.

Wire brush, why not a chicken?

You may think I jest here, but I am serious. Wire brushes may indeed be used in certain instances — but only on oak or ash.

I demonstrated this technique one time to a woodworking class and they couldn't believe what I was doing or why I needed to, or, was I in fact, crazy? Well, I suppose this is arguable, but not where this technique is concerned.

When you want to clean all the dust from the wood, not just the surface stuff, a wire brush is the tool to use.

A wire brush will remove all unwanted dust from the deepest pores of oak or ash because the wood is tough enough to take it. This can be seen in the lower photo below. On the right side of the photo is the wood just after sanding. You can dust off the wood with your trusty dust brush, but you are only going to get rid of the surface dust.

On the left side of the picture, the wire brush has been used and the pores have been cleaned — if only it could have been this easy for me when I was a kid with acne! You will also discover that the wood will feel smoother after using this wire brush technique.

Try doing that with a chicken!

Full of fillers

There are lots of fillers out there. One particular filler, who's name shall remain nameless, is the bane of the re-finisher because inevitably, when stripping, he will come across this petrified stuff, which cannot be dated and must be hacked away by pick axe or, as a last resort, nitro — which is quite self-defeating because the furniture is usually destroyed in the explosion and what you have left you use for firewood.

I say this of course in a highly exaggerated mode because, well, aside from minor surface irregularities, filler and putties need only be used sparingly.

I once took care of an end table from the 1940s. The person who had brought it to my shop was unaware that one-third of the upper portion of one leg was comprised of the above un-named putty. The stripping process revealed the truth.

I once stripped a door and found, to my amazement, that in the 3" hole where the knob had once been was completely filled with what seemed like maybe three or four cans of the same stuff — stuffed, packed and smoothed into the hole. I suppose it speaks highly of said material's longevity and durability, but I think you will agree that putty hardly serves as a substitute for wood.

Let's just take a simple nail hole for example. You putty the hole and then what? You have to wait for the putty to dry.

2 Finally, when the putty has dried, you put down *War and Peace* and you sand. If you have not been efficient when applying your putty, which it to say if you didn't remove the excess after filling the hole, you are going to wind up sanding and sanding and sanding.

3 So, rather than sanding in that one lonely spot for however long it may take, and, if the putty that you used is solvent-based (Famowood is a popular wood filler which is acetone-based), you can use a piece of No.0000 steel wool dipped in a bit of solvent to remove the excess which reduces the sanding time and gets you back to the Bolsheviks that much quicker.

Fill holes with colored wax sticks

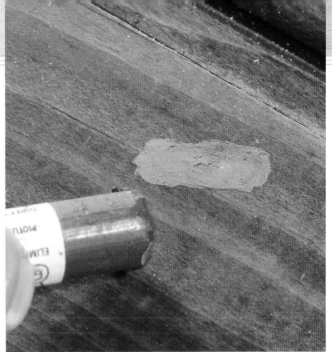

I What I usually do is wait until the entire job is finished and fill any and all nail holes with the appropriately colored wax or putty stick.

It doesn't take an Einstein to master this — in fact, Einstein couldn't wax-fill to save his life. (Marconi. Now there was a wax-filler.) All you have to do is find the appropriate color fill stick.

2 Rub the stick back and forth over the nail or other hole.

3 Rub away the excess with a piece of terry cloth towel or cheesecloth.

Fill in for fill sticks

I was in a house finishing up my job of replacing all the baseboards in the downstairs living room. The wood had been prefinished, thereby preventing any chance of drips occurring which is always a certainty when finishing is done in place. All I had to do was cart the pre-finished boards to the job, cut and install and "Bob's your uncle". Naturally, something is always left behind. That day I'd neglected to pack my fill sticks — and I had a whole new box I had just gotten from the finishing supply house. There were obvious nail holes I'd made in the baseboards and I didn't really want to have to come back just to fill holes.

The nanny in charge of the two kids had let me know she would be taking the kids to the park, so, once they'd gone, I made my way into the kid's playroom and found exactly what I'd hoped to find. There on the Arts & Crafts table sat a plastic container full of childhood in the form and smell of crayons! I quickly searched the booty for brown and a black, took them, got back to the living room and — Presto!

The perfect fill in for fill sticks.

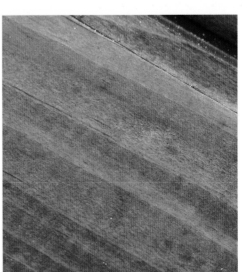

4 Mission accomplished Einstein.

Get steamed

Sometimes a hunk of something just happens to fall on what you've built. And it's usually the top that gets it, right? Well, there's a simple way to get rid of bruises such as this without resorting to what has just been discussed a page ago, namely, filling holes and dents with putty.

Now understand, I am only talking about minor dents and dings. Maybe your hammer falls on the surface you've just spent six hours tending to.

An impact such as this will naturally leave a mark.

Or, let's say you're moving the piece from one room to the next and, in turning it through the doorway, you hit the jamb (like I'm making believe to do in the picture) which scores the top, side or edge resulting in an abrasion or dent. These are minor. Get what I'm saying? I'm not talking about a rock slide, a lightning strike or a rogue asteroid.

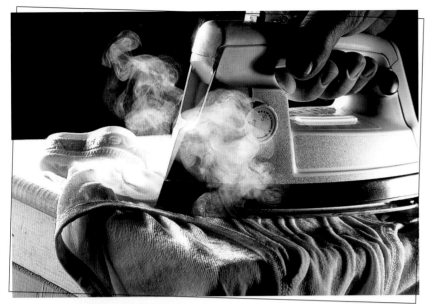

The way to remedy this, especially before the wood has been finished (because once there's finish on the wood it's that much more difficult), is with steam. Naturally, the perfect tool to use is the steam iron. All you have to do is lay a damp cloth over the dent and place the hot iron on the cloth.

The steam will swell the wood and bring it back to level. This will work wonders on pine, poplar and mahogany. However, the denser the wood, the more steam is needed, and sometimes, depending on just how severe the wood fibres have been crushed, it may be impossible to remove the dent unless you and a friend drag the damaged piece to Old Faithful at Yellowstone (bottom photo). This simple formula for removing dents applies to anything you can construct from wood.

In closing this chapter I'd just like to say that everything thus said about wood prep is about time, luck, patience and skill. And all you have to do is remember that time is on your side unless you choose otherwise, luck you either have or don't, patience isn't necessarily virtuous and skill is what comes from repeated doing.

Now go sand something — or turn to the next chapter.

3

starting to Finish

Knowing when to stain or, when not to stain is purely a matter of feeling and vision. Some people slap the same stain on everything, others may slap on stuff they know little or nothing about and then slap themselves or the person next to them when it turns out looking like the thing in the dream that had been chasing them.

I think you will agree that knowing what you want the work to look like is first and foremost. (And no — that is not William Shatner holding my brushes. It's me, doing my Shatner impersonation.)

A stain by any other name is still messy

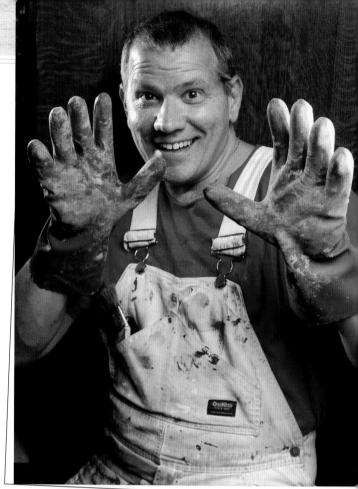

What stain you choose to use for your particular project is completely up to you, and — as limited as you are by buying from the shelf of the hardware store or home center — there is still a large selection of colors you can choose from to achieve a variety of effects with very little effort.

Before going on about stains, a basic point: Any paint can be thinned down to make a stain-like coating to color wood.

Perhaps the most easily recognizable of finishes where this method is employed would be the *pickled look*. Just what is the pickled look? (Not counting my Uncle's look after he's lost the tri-fecta!) The pickled look is achieved by using a basic white paint which has been thinned with a reasonable amount of thinner (or water, if latex paint is being used), and brushing the resulting liquid on the wood. The excess is then removed as any other stain would be removed — by wiping with a rag or paper towels. This technique is usually most effective when done to oak or ash and, in some cases, pine. (See chapter four, In a Pickle, Whitewash on Oak or Pine.)

The point I am making, and the point is pretty obvious, is that something is being brushed on and wiped off, thereby coloring the wood.

I don't care what color paint: brown, blue, green, red — whatever you like — the paint can be thinned, applied, wiped off and then coated with clear finish. You could find a roofer, get him to give you some tar, thin it with gasoline, which will create a deep, black stain, as the gasoline will break down the tar to an almost-paint, which may then be brushed onto wood, thereby coloring it.

Think of it. You could play ancient Egyptian and coat and preserve your own mummies!

Am I advocating tar finishes?

Not at all, folks. I merely state that lots of things, even something like tar (that you would hardly expect to incorporate into finishing), may be used to color wood. In fact, way back when, during colonial times and further back still, one of the major ingredients for certain milk-paint coatings was animal blood!

Penetrating oil stains

The word penetrating, although somewhat incorrect, may be used with the understanding that what is penetrating is the solvent, while the coloring aspect (or pigment) in the stain tends to lay on top of the wood rather than enter it.

At the bottom of any can of oil-stain you will feel the pigment that has settled there (see photo at right). The manufacturer recommends stirring but I think you should also try applying the liquid before agitating the sludge. You may find some stains contain an overabundance of pigment and, in applying it to the wood, leaves a heavy pigment coating that obscures the grain a little too much. In this case you may have to wipe some of the pigment away with a rag that has been soaked with paint thinner. This is why it's important to always do tests on scrap wood first.

I can't say this enough.

My goal was not to compile a book that contained page after page of pictures of blocks of wood displaying what various combinations of colors can look like.

After all, there are swatches from the manufacturer readily available on the stain shelves at the home center to show you what each color looks like. I'd rather leave this endeavour up to the curious — those eager types who get bit by the finishing bug and live to experiment with colors — locked away in their garage or basement workshop and then, at the dinner table, passing the rolls, their fingers multi-colored. (Be sure to wear rubber or vinyl gloves for this particular reason.)

I want to encourage you to experiment with different stains by taking you step by step through a combination of stains for a particular treatment that I have used on oak, as well as walnut and mahogany, for years without fail.

I believe this to be much more beneficial to the novice than looking at pictures of wood with different stains on them, along with lists of proportions and combinations, without showing how they're utilized. Basically, it comes down to experimenting, so be adventurous. Go get yourself some half-pint cans of stain and get to work.

SAFETY TIP

Whenever you are working with solvent-based products — whether oil stains, varnishes, lacquer or polyurethane — it's good to have either an explosion-proof can (available from woodworking supply stores) or a bucket with some water in it. Solvent-based products have been known to spontaneously ignite.

DOES IT MATTER WHICH STAIN I USE?

As far as which stain to use, remember, if you're using a water-based stain, you can apply a solvent-based varnish, polyurethane or lacquer, on top. However, if you are using an oil stain, be sure to read the label to see if you can top coat with water-based clear finishes.

If the label doesn't specify, it's probably okay but you should allow several days or even a week for the stain to dry to be on the safe side.

Joe's old-world finish

Red mahogany on oak

Special walnut on oak

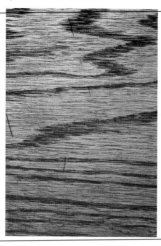

Golden oak on oak

Yuck! I never liked red mahogany on oak by itself, which is the reason for this particular old-world finish. By the way, if you are ever in Philadelphia, check out Downey's restaurant at Front and South. Here you can see for yourself the raw-bar (where they serve the oysters and clams) that I not only finished utilizing this recipe, but also distressed so that it more matched the original existing bar which had been brought over from Ireland.

The wood is dark, but not that attractive. In fact, it appears kind of lifeless. This stain alone, applied to oak and viewed under fluorescent light is frightening, due to the fact that fluorescent light kills any warm, red tones in the color spectrum — in furniture as well as flesh — and no one ever sees themselves as looking good under fluorescent light, with the exception, maybe, of Michael Jackson.

I think you will agree there's nothing particularly special here, yet people will buy these stains and do what comes naturally, which is to open the can, apply it to the wood, wipe it away and brush on a poly.

End of story.

And this is all fine and well, but with a bit more finesse, once can excel in the miraculous. If you combine these three stains to affect a finish on oak you arrive at what you see in the picture below.

Notice how the oak now exhibits a warmer feeling? This feeling cannot be achieved by merely coating wood with a single oil stain of any color — especially on new wood. You can see what I mean it when I say it seems an awful shame that anyone who would spend so many hours building something would want to slap a single coat of anything on what they've made and call it quits, unless, of course, they just want to get it over with and jump on to the next project.

Each of the oil stains mentioned above were applied. Each succeeding coat of stain was followed by a sealer coat of shellac: 1 part shellac, 5 parts denatured alcohol (in Canada or England, it's referred to as methyl hydrate).

Because oak is deeply porous, you can put several coatings on it. This process becomes trickier when you try it on woods such as maple, birch or cherry, do to the density of the woods and the tightness of the pores.

So, here's the recipe, all laid out for use on any newly constructed and sanded oak project. Or, for use on stripped and sanded oak.

The Process

1 Apply the first stain. Wipe off the excess and allow to dry. Apply a shellac wash (sealer) coat. If the wash-coat step is not followed, there's a chance that the second coat of stain will pull off the first, or at least lighten it considerably.

2 Sand with 320-grit silicon-carbide paper. This is a single-pass, very light sanding on flat surfaces only. I like to use a used piece of paper — not one right out of the sleeve — as this will be too rough. You want to be careful so that you do not scratch into the stain.

3 Apply the second stain. Wipe the excess from surface and allow the stain to dry. Applying the second stain is much easier than applying the first. It's like applying a second coat of paint — it's always quicker than the first coat. Stain is the same. Once the stain is dry, apply a second wash-coat of shellac. This takes practice but you will get the hang of it soon enough. Be careful. If you brush too much in one spot you're going to pull off the first coat of shellac and create light spots.

4 Repeat step 2. Use the used sandpaper once again for this step and then dust off. Notice my fingers holding the paper the way I outlined in the wood-prep chapter? They follow the grain of the wood and my middle knuckles look like freshly made tortellini.

5 With the wood lightly sanded as outlined in step 4, apply your third and final coat of stain and allow it to dry. When the third coat of stain is dry, shellac everything a third time remembering not to over-brush and pull up what you've already laid down.

The best applied stains are those where you do not see any smear marks, as we shall soon learn in the pages that follow. I suggest practicing wiping stain from wood in all sorts of ways because this is where the real art comes in — and I'm not talking about flat pieces of wood either — I'm talking about honest-to-goodness real furniture. Remember, if, after you've applied a stain and you've botched it, all you have to do is wash it down with paint thinner and start again. It'a a pain, I agree, but it's not the end of the world.

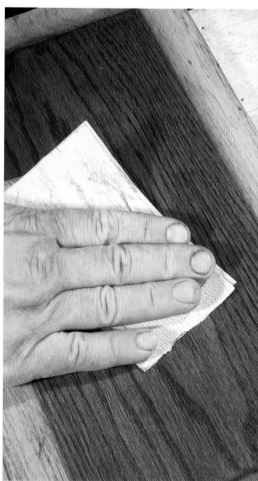

6 Repeat step two again. Alright, here's the final, light sanding...fingers barely brushing the surface of shellac...treat it gently... easy does it.

7 Now, all you have to do is use a tack rag to remove the sanding dust and lay on the topcoat of your choice. You can apply varnish, Varathane or lacquer. DO NOT use polyurethane. It will not stick to this stain sandwich. Make sure that all steps have included lots of drying time between each step. (Note: You may find that foam brushes help in applying varnishes as they are less likely to leave rough hairs or brush marks in your finish.)

You may also mix the above three stains together in whatever proportion you wish and apply three coats of that mixture, following the seven step outlined previously.

The mix could be, for example, one-third red mahogany, one-third special walnut and one-third golden oak. But, whatever proportions you choose will work.

APPLYING FINISH ON THE LEVEL

When applying any type of poly, lacquer or other topcoat, it's important that the surface — especially large surfaces — is level.

If the surface is not level, you are going to run into problems, because wherever the surface dips, the finish is going to gather and create a mess. So check for level both ways.

For instance, the top of a bureau may be level but the floor may be off. Applying the level north-south then east-west and shimming accordingly at the bottom of the bureau will assure an even, flat cure.

Problem areas

Don't fret the sweat

I would like to cover a variety of fears people often have when working with oil stains.

When the weather is a factor, you can run into problems. If oil stain is applied in cold weather, the stain will take a long time to dry, and you will wind up with a tacky mess that never seems to dry. As a result, all kinds of air-born particulate matter and tiny bugs collect on the wet surface. When the weather is hot with high humidity, the oil stain will be inhibited from drying in a different way in that moisture from the air settling on top of the applied oil stain will cause the pores of the wood to "sweat." (Top photo at right.)

When the stain continues to sweat from the pores of the wood after you've wiped away the excess, remember to keep tending to those areas where the sweating is occurring by continuing to wipe wherever the stain shows itself. This can literally take hours — it's like you are on watch. Be sure to have a book to read with you. If you walk away and let it dry, you will have to wipe away the dots of oozed dried stain with some burlap and paint thinner. (Middle photo at right.) Doing this will result in a light spot in the stained wood that will be nearly impossible to cover up. You should clean all the remaining stain from the wood and start all over, rather than attempt to apply stain to these areas. Choose your staining days carefully.

Let's put it this way — if you overhear people saying "it's not the heat, it's the humidity" — don't stain with oil-based products on that day.

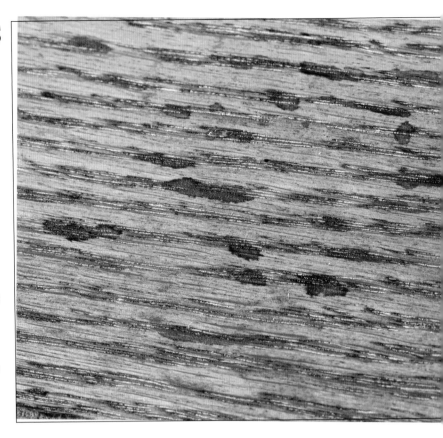

Fear of drying

Another problem is the fear of the stain drying before you have had time to wipe the excess from the wood. This kind of panic only encourages the nefarious smears due to improper wiping.

Let's look at the first problem, which is not a problem at all, merely beginner's anxiety.

Say you start at the left end of a chest of drawers and work your way over to the right, then do the drawer fronts, then the mirror frame, etc. When you get back to where you began and start to wipe the excess stain away with a rag or some paper towels, you discover the stuff has begun to dry!

The towels are sticking!

It's a mess!

"YAAAAAAAAAAAAAAA!"

Relax.

All you have to do is take a clump of paper towels that are wet with stain (see photo at right), (the clump you've already used will work just fine) and brush more stain onto the chest of drawers. Then wipe away the excess wet stain.

Take this mass of wet paper towels and begin to rub the surfaces of the wood. Lo and behold, wherever the stain seemed to be dry has now become re-activated by the stain-wet paper towels and your careful rubbing. You are able to see on the left and right sides of this picture the darkness of the stain that has begun to set up and dry. I am wearing a vinyl glove and the towel that I am using is thoroughly wet with stain.

Moving the wet towel parallel to the grain creates an even look. You must be consistent. You can't expect to wipe away evenly if you're making like you're wiping a window pane with Windex. This is a controlled movement. Pay attention. Granted, it's easier when you're working with a flat piece of wood, but like I said, the more you do something the better you're going to get at doing it.

Fear of smears

Smears created from improper wiping, like improper sanding, can only be controlled by being aware of how your arm is moving. Because of the way our arms are constructed — wrist bone to elbow, elbow to shoulder — it is perfectly natural to make the motion of a windshield wiper.

Try it. Hold your arm out in front of you, elbow bent, back of your hand facing your face and go left and go right like you're waving bye like Jed Clampett at the end of a Beverley Hillbillies TV show. It's the way our bones move, so during times of sanding and wiping stain from wood surfaces, you need to be conscious of how your arm is moving and that you're not making this all-too-easy movement. In the photo at right, you can see how careless wiping when staining will create curved smears on the wood, which are easily wiped away if you move your arm in the direction of the wood grain.

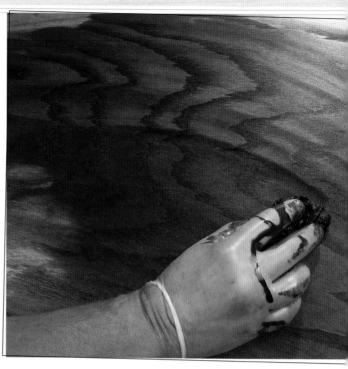

Sandpaper scratches

Being careless when sanding will create severe problems because you will scar the wood with arcs of sandpaper scratches that will only show up more with the application of stain.

Dry brushing

This dry-brush technique is great for dabbing excess stain from out of carved mouldings, spindles or any kind of crack or crevice.

Gotcha blotch!

Another type of smear is more of a blotch. For example, when you're wiping into a corner where two baseboards meet. (Photo at left.)

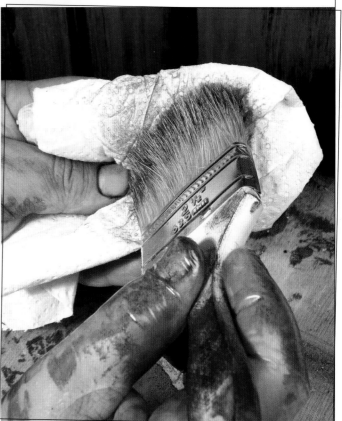

Try as you may, sometimes you can't get a straight wipe, so you have these spots where it looks like the beginnings of a faux marble finish. Here's what to do. Get yourself a dry bristle brush (I'm using a cheap throw-away brush), get into those corners and pull the stain away, starting from the bottom and working your way up if it's a vertical surface.

Naturally, if you are working on a baseboard, for example, which runs horizontal, you want to pull the brush left or right parallel to the floor.

You'll need to dab the bristles of the brush on some paper towels to blot away the stain from the bristles as you go along. Notice that I have my trusty vinyl gloves on — well I do on one hand at least.

Gel stains

Gel stains are just what they sound like: jelly.

For those over forty, I would say think of them as having the consistency of Dippity Do, that wonderful hair gel from the 1960s, while those younger would more identify with the consistency of Jello Pudding. (Inset photo.)

Gel stains are pigment suspended in oil that are whipped to a certain thickness. You need not stir, they don't smell nearly as much as other oil stains and they won't drip. They'll glop if you drop some to the floor, but they won't drip or sweat after they've been applied. Also, gel stains will not spatter from the working of the brush.

I can remember working frantically on a piece and spattering myself several times to where I looked like I do in the photo at right. I became so involved in the work that I wound up leaving my shop, forgetting, of course, to clean the stuff from my face. Back then it was real stain, here I simply used chocolate syrup, as Hitchcock did for the nefarious shower scene in Psycho.

Gels work well for staining woods such as cherry, birch and pine because they lay on top of the wood instead of entering the wood.

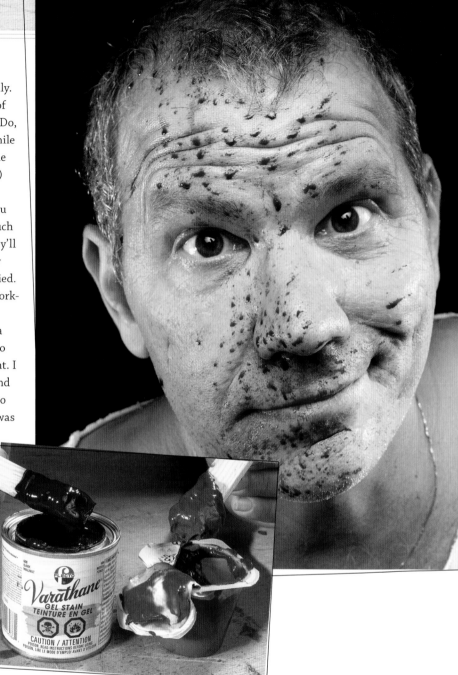

Paper towels are ideal for wiping stain from wood. Rags can leave microscopic fibers attached to the wood grain — especially on deep-grained woods like oak, ash and mahogany. These fibers will not be visible until you have applied a clear finish.

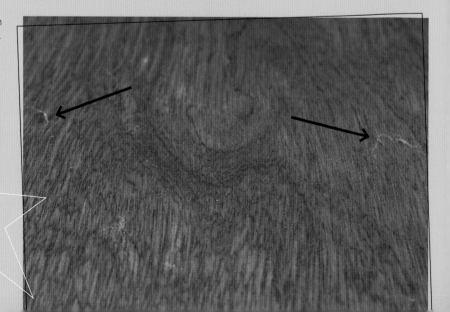

Water-based stains

Here we are again with water-based stains.

I mentioned earlier how much easier the cleanup procedure is with water-based stains and how they cause the problem of grain raising. While there are a sizable amount of color choices, walnuts, mahoganies, pines and so forth, many seem to fall in the green, blue, and grey range of designer-like colors. I don't know how suitable these colors are for furniture, they're there for experimenting with at your leisure.

When discussing oil stains, I explained how panic is libel to set in if the stain you are using begins to set up or appears to be drying on the wood before you've had time to wipe off the excess. I also explained how easy it is to reactivate the stain by simply applying more stain. Not so with water-based stains. There is a minimum of about three minutes before water-based stains set up and dry, so you must work fast. Remember to choose your stain according to the size of the job.

Experience is knowing what product is going to give the most satisfying results and less trouble over   all, not necessarily the one that is going to be a no-muss clean up.

Consider an ordinary run-of-the-mill pine or oak nightstand. I would, or could, and have, used water-based stains and have managed to attain great results finishing something like this. In fact, it is possible to apply two coats (sand between coats) of water-based stain sealed with a couple of coats of de-waxed shellac, and then to top coat everything with two coats of lacquer or water-based polyurethane in a single day — providing the weather conditions are favorable. This many steps in a row and in the same day would be nearly impossible feat with oil-based products, even with the cooperation of the weather. But I would never attempt staining a large wall unit with water-based stain unless I was able to work with the speed of Tobor-the-8th Man. I'd only be inviting trouble.

Oil-based stain on cherry

This is the effect when an oil-based stain is applied to bare cherry wood. You can see, especially in the wavy grain lines in the right of the photo, how they appear exaggerated and dark.

Water-based gel stain on cherry

This is the effect of a gel stain that has been applied to bare cherry wood. The gel stain lays on top of the wood rather than entering it, so there is less splotching, which results in a more even finish.

PREPARATION FOR WATER-BASED FINISHES OR DON'T RAISE MY GRAIN

In order to achieve as smooth a finish as possible when using water-based top coatings — with the understanding that water-based finishes will raise the grain of wood — it is necessary to reduce the amount of grain the finish is going to raise by wetting and then sanding the dry wood before applying the finish.

Sponge the surface of the wood with a damp sponge — not soaking wet — and allow the wood to dry. When dry, you will feel the surface is rough. This is the surface as it would feel if this step was neglected, except that the finish will have dried on top of it. It would then be difficult, if not impossible, to arrive at a smooth effect, even after rigorous rubbing to buff the dry film. Wet to raise and sand to smooth. How many times is your choice.

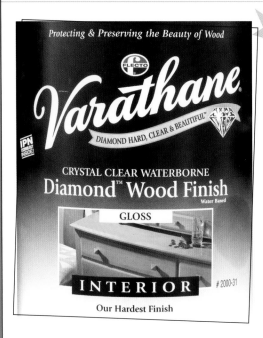

Water-based clear finishes

Water-based clear finishes have overtaken the shelves. Good or bad? I'd say, just like our planet and it's inhabitants, there's room for everyone. All finishes can and should be used because *there is no perfect finish.*

I couldn't begin to count the number of people I've met over the years, while doing personal appearances and seminars, that have wanted to know what the best finish is for their project — as if I could tell them where to find a particular brand on the shelf that says *the best finish.* Rather than thinking *best finish,* perhaps the mindset of the buyer should be: how well is the finish being used or applied.

There are a lot of great finishes which translates to many finishing possibilities. The important thing is to learn how to deduce what finish is going to work best for your particular project. If you don't mind the fact that water-based finishes raise the grain of the wood, add another step before you even start, their flat and somewhat dull finish-film left behind and the non-reflective resulting look — go ahead and use a water-based finish. I have used water-based polyurethane on several maple jobs that needed to look as natural as possible and, because the water-based finish rendered the look I was after, it became the product I deemed necessary to use.

I have found occasion to use water-based finishes on everything but the tops of desks, bureaus and the like, preferring to finish the tops of these types of furniture with lacquer or varnish in order to be able to rub the tops out to a satiny smooth finish.

My major concern with water-based polyurethanes and varnishes for top surfaces is that they are unable to be rubbed out and polished successfully. Also, they can be affected by the weather — just like oil-based products. They are no more heat, water or acid resistant than lacquer — even on tabletops.

Rust from the dust

You should be aware — and this really gets me going — that there are people out there in woodworking land who refuse to use sandpaper and choose steel wool as the abrasive of choice for sanding between coats of clear finish and then wonder why they haven't been able to achieve a smooth finish.

Steel wool is not going to give the surface enough of a scuff or *tooth,* for the next coat of finish. Don't get me wrong, steel wool is great stuff and an abrasive for sure, but, it's best for polishing final finishes — not for prep work between coats of clear finish, especially when you are dealing with grain that has been raised by water-based products. Steel wool cannot get rid of the surface bumps of the particulate matter that has fallen onto and dried in the varnish or polyurethane.

You must use finishing sandpaper.

Abrading a dried coat of water-based finish with steel wool before re-coating can be problematic. If you fail to get all the steel wool dust from the surface, the dust can be trapped between layers of finish and specks of black spots may appear in the finish. Not so bad if it's dark wood, but on a natural oak or maple surface? There's nothing you can do to get rid of these annoying little specs except strip the work down to the bare wood, apply bleach if there are any residual stains in the wood — or apply a large doily and a vase containing the flower of choice.

Use sandpaper between finish coats!

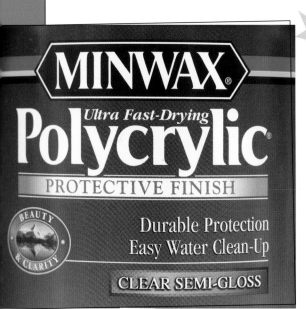

Talk and no one listens

I once dated a woman who fancied herself a know-it-all when it came to all things paintable. She was supposedly an expert, and, while she was as good a painter of ceilings as I have ever met, she knew nothing at all about the materials. It is important for me to relay this tale because it proves what I have been saying all along, namely, that you need to know what is compatible with what, otherwise you're headed for disaster.

Her job was to paint and marbleize two, 6½'-tall, 10"-diameter columns. Marbling was something she did adequately enough, and she used latex paint. Fine. Once the paint had dried, she then wanted to clear-coat the surfaces of the columns to make them glossy, thereby creating the illusion of true polished marble. Great.

I suggested she use a water-based polyurethane, given the fact that both it and latex paint are made up of the same material base and because water-based clear-coat dries crystal clear, they would not alter the color of her faux finish. Oil-based varnish or polyurethane is slightly amber in color and would affect the colors of the faux finish.

But no! She had to go pick someone else's brain for a solution. She went to an art supply store and was given the wrong advice — and made to suffer for it. The salesman convinced her to use a clear topcoat that was xylene based. "Ultimate in gloss" he'd said, so she told me over the sobs I could hear as I pressed the phone to my ear. Xylene, as I reported earlier in chapter one (if you didn't bypass that section), is notorious for dissolving water-based finishes. The product Goof Off is xylene based and marketed specifically to house painters and homeowners for the quick and easy removal of spattered latex paint on floors and such. What happened to her handiwork as she brushed the stuff onto her faux-finished columns was that the surfaces of paint started to crackle — and continued to crack and crack.

But, you see, I often talk to myself.

End grain

Oil stain applied to end grain will always be darker. Most of you don't even notice this detail because you never see the difference. The way to even things out is to apply some shellac to the end grain before staining. Allow the shellac to dry and then lightly sand. Now when you stain, you will get a more even effect.

On the right side of the photo you can clearly discern how the stain has soaked into the wood. Why? Because end grain is extremely porous.

To the left of the dark side (ha ha), you have the power of (dare I say it?) the Force of Shellac, as it has limited the absorption of the stain.

Anytime you have end grain and you want a more even stain, remember to apply some shellac straight from the can with the appropriate-width brush, allow it to dry and then sand with 220- or 320-grit sandpaper.

Be sure the stain you have applied is completely dry before you apply the clear finish over oil-based penetrating stains. If you don't, two things could happen. Either the clear finish will pull off the stain, or, the clear finish will not dry properly — your choice.

Silicone infection

Silicone infection is caused by oils, grease, anything your fingers touch and then touch the wood — even things that may have be placed on the wood in the wood's distant past can cause the dreaded silicone infection.

When silicones are present in the wood, you will find that the finish puckers (photo below) thereby preventing the finish to level out as it should. The main cause of silicone infection is caused by spray-on polishes that actually contain silicones. It is the silicones in the spray, you see, that makes the polishing aspect that much easier.

Good for you, bad for the wood.

The sample I made for this demonstration was achieved by spraying a raw piece of wood with a spray polish containing silicones. Wood that has been stripped of its old finish can become contaminated in the stripping process if silicone polishes were ever used on the surface. The finish comes off, true, but the silicone is simply spread about and redeposited on the wood.

Already six or seven years into paying my dues as a finisher, I wasn't aware of these silicone infections. Never saw it, let alone knew how to take care of it, even though I had been taking care of it without even knowing I was taking care of it.

Makes no sense at all right?

Well, I meant it to sound that way. Let me explain.

In the beginning, and by this I mean when I started, I would finish everything as outlined in "Joe's Old-World Finish." (See page 58.)

My finish always incorporated three coats of oil stain sandwiched between three spit-coats of orange shellac, followed by three coats of brushed on crystal varnish (sanded between coats, naturally). The only variation was in the color, or colors of oil stain I used. What I didn't know was that by shellacking the wood between coats of stain I was preventing the pucker effect from ever occurring.

My discovery of silicone infection came one day when I had taken on the job of stripping and refinishing a 5' by 7' kitchen table made of old mahogany boards. It was a thick table that had, in fact, been built by a former employer.

I stripped what finish remained on the surface and then set out to coat the wood with a spar varnish, which is what I had taken off the wood, and which my former employer had always insisted be applied to everything. (Not that I was hearing him still shouting orders to me that many years later, no, I simply felt that seeing as how my client was using this table as his kitchen table, which, inevitably was going to be exposed to moisture, and, knowing spar, or, marine varnish is well employed in these kinds of cases, I decided to use the stuff.)

The first stroke of varnish I laid down puckered immediately. I said some things I can't write here, and then said more unprintable things again and again. I didn't know what to think or, quite frankly, what to do. I did notice that if I dragged the brush over the applied varnish, the puckering would smooth out, only to reappear as quickly. What to do? I had no Internet. I didn't even know what to call it in order to ask someone. So I went to a local how-to bookstore (this was in 1986), and found a book that talked about what I was faced with. The book was titled *Finishing Technology* by George A. Soderberg. (A book I still own.) This book was an actual textbook on finishing wood, metal and other things — with actual questions and answers at the end of each chapter!

And, because I'd never heard about silicone infection, I couldn't just turn to the index to find the solution, so I stood

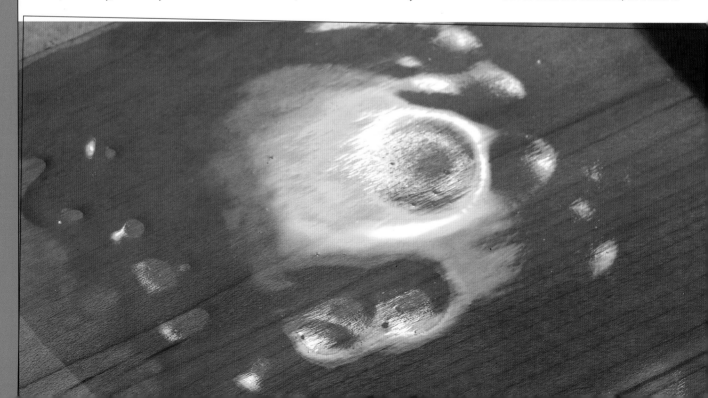

there turning the pages of the book in the aisle of that slightly cramped store until, at the bottom right corner of page 131, I came upon a picture of exactly what it was I had come face to face with myself in the shop. The text under the picture read *Fish Eyes*, which appeared in the newly applied varnish coat showing the presence of silicone.

It mentioned fisheye (the industry name for the problem) and flowout (drops) to correct the fisheye, but I didn't know where to purchase these, and what's more, I needed to get the table finished and out of my shop. As I read further it mentioned washing the wood with toluene, xylene or turpentine. When I stripped the top, I had used lacquer thinner in the process and did my final wash with paint thinner, which, unlike turpentine, is a petroleum distillate, but to no avail. I'd try turpentine when I got back, I thought.

I bought the book ($20). The washing with turpentine didn't work. The surface still puckered. Then I tried shellac, which the book said would act as a barrier coat between the infection and the finish, realizing, finally, at that moment, why I had never experienced this problem before — because I had always used shellac on everything!

Problem solved.

However, even after applying a spit coat of shellac to the wood my varnish still puckered — especially around some rather long check marks. No. The finish would just not gather. I checked the book again, and I quote: "A poultice composed of fuller's earth or some other absorbent clay may be placed over

Fisheye Flowout has an additive that will combat silicone contamination. I add 8 to 10 drops per quart of varnish or lacquer when I finish stripped furniture.

the break to dissolve and absorb the silicone. Removal of the clay after it is dry will further remove more of the silicone."

One block from my shop, a group of city guys were tearing up the street. They were depositing large piles of yellow clay all around the sides of the hole they were digging, so I asked if I could take a few buckets. They said yes, so I helped myself. Using some chicken wire, I sifted through three buckets of yellow clay, getting rid of all bits of glass, rocks and pebbles until I had earth. Good old terra firma in powder form.

I mixed this sifted earth with water and smeared this on the washed-clean mahogany and let it sit overnight. After removing the dried clay and washing the wood down with xylene (which I'd since gone out and purchased), I lightly sanded the wood (as the poultice had raised the grain) and then applied my varnish.

Low and behold! Not a single pucker save for a single incidental scar along one of the check marks in the wood, which, after rubbing out with some steel wool and wax was hardly discernible in the final finish.

The reason I have gone on at length to describe this problem and it's remedy is to reassure you that there is always a solution. It may take a while before you come upon it, but perseverance always pays off.

Dewaxed shellac

What are commonly referred to, in the business, as shellac flakes are just what you see glittering in my hand and on the table in the photo above.

These can be purchased by mail order in 1- or 5-pound bags as well as a from a well-stocked art supply store or woodworking supply houses. The dry form of shellac comes in many varieties such as seedlac, which is the least refined, buttonlac, which offers a browner, more amber tone than ordinary amber shellac and super blonde, which is the highest grade of refinement and is dewaxed.

The reason for the dewaxing is for adhesion purposes. Dewaxed shellac will accept succeeding topcoats of varnish or lacquer better than plain shellac. All this said, understand that the wax is a natural ingredient in the shellac flake.

In ready-made form, the Zinsser Company, in addition to their clear and amber shellac, make Seal-Coat, which is 100% shellac that is dewaxed — so it can be used between coats of water-based or oil-based stains.

When you make your own liquid shellac, you can separate the wax from the rest of the mix. Fill a jar with shellac flakes and cover the flakes with alcohol. Allow this to sit overnight, and, in the morning, so help me, you will see a cloudy residue at the bottom of the jar, while the top portion will look like a nice brew of lemon iced tea. This is the dewaxed part.

Do not dare drink this instead of your coffee.

The cloudy muck at the bottom is the wax you don't want. Using a small scoop or ladel, pull the top liquid from the jar, strain it and you have your dewaxed shellac.

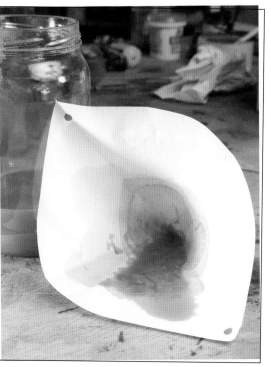

Whether you need to dewax your shellac or not is your call. If you just want to dissolve some flakes to make regular shellac, be sure to strain the stuff through a fine mesh cone strainer.

Using a strainer will separate the solids from the disolved shellac crystals.

The art supply store

Leaving the home center, we visit the art supply store. You can find a lot of great things in an art supply store — a lot of strange people too — if you are so inclined. Naturally, some may say it's not necessary, while others may be interested in what these items may help you create in your woodworking finishes.

Artists oil tubes

In Chapter one I spoke about how I had stained a desk I'd purchased using a single tube of burnt umber artist's oil color and some paint thinner. Why? Because they are oil colors, and I know that in conjunction with paint thinner, the color can be thinned, applied and wiped off just like any other stain. Artist's colors are invaluable when there is nothing else available. Buy some tubes and keep them around for those times when you need to color something but can't get to the home center.

Add these colors to your arsenal of finishing supplies: Burnt umber, Van Dyke Brown, yellow ochre, raw sienna, burnt sienna, titanium white, ivory and black.

Imagine these two colors mixed and thinned — you can see how it would work as an appropriate stain for oak, maple or pine.

Japan colors

These products are invaluable for finishing wood. I literally couldn't do without them. Japan colors are made from finely ground pigments suspended in oil and can be mixed with varnishes and lacquers for all kinds of glazing effects and accents. They dry dull and can be top coated with varnish or lacquer. They can be added to oil stains for heightened tonal qualities, or thinned with paint thinner or turpentine. Go that extra distance and find them — but you don't have to go to Japan — just the local art supply store.

In the chart at right, you can see the variety of colors that are available — deep blues, oranges, reds, forest greens, as well as burnt umber, raw and burnt sienna — which are earth colors and essential to wood finishing.

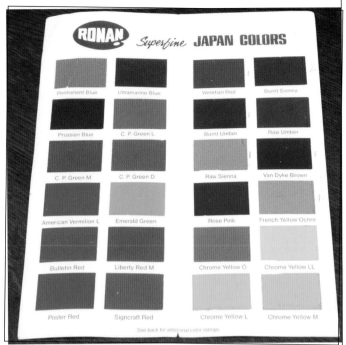

Tempera colors

Every school kid knows what these are. They're safe, non-toxic and, in a pinch, they can be used as a stain or used for detail work. (See Chapter 2, Edge Treatment.) The nice thing about these colors is that they come in a variety of colors. These paints dry fast and can be sealed and/or topcoated with shellac.

Dry pigments

Artist's oil tube paint is made of dry pigment and linseed oil. What you see in this photo is a lovely group shot of natural pigments.

In essence, these are pure color without carrier, binder or driers. They can be mixed with shellac, lacquer or varnish and used for touch-up work. In a pinch, you can color bare spots and even entire surfaces if you are lacking in other supplies for the job. (see Chapter 4, Strictly Stickley.) Yellow ochre, burnt umber, raw umber, burnt sienna, white, cadmium red and black are good to start with. Buy some and place them next to your artist's oil tubes — because the tubes are going to get lonely!

Varnish brushes

I don't care what quality of paint brush you can find at the home center or hardware store, they will be nothing like the reliable varnish brushes you can find at the local art supply store. 1", 2" and 3" widths are best. But, the photo shows you how many shapes and varieties are actually available. Keep these clean at all times and they will live a long life.

Disposable pallets

Disposable pallets are good for mixing paint (see Chapter 4, Albert's "bar job"), and are nothing more than booklets of heavy wax paper. In fact, you can probably go to a dollar store and find pads of finger-paint paper which are basically the same thing. That's what I do.

Fine brushes

Fine brushes are necessary for touch-up work. At the art supply store you can find synthetic hair or nylon bristle brushes for water-based products as well as hair brushes for oils.

Tips

Container with handle

Don't throw anything away — that's my motto. These containers are great for use with shellac, paint, varnish or lacquer. All that needs be done is to cut away the front section, clean out the inside with a bit of alcohol, wipe with fresh towels and you're ready to pour.

Cleaning aerosol can tips

Many times the tips or nozzles of spray cans can get clogged and the paint, varnish or shellac winds up spitting all over the place when you press down, or, nothing comes out at all.

Place the nozzles into a small container of lacquer thinner and let them sit overnight. This usually works. If not, something else is wrong with the can.

Plumber's tape on jar assures easy open

This is a good tip for shellac jars. If the rim of a shellac jar becomes coated with shellac and the lid is tightened, it's going to be tough to unscrew. Sometimes plastic explosives are necessary.

I have had to submerge the top in a container of alcohol to soften the dry shellac. Here, wrapping the screw rim with plumber's Teflon tape assures the lid will unscrew easily.

I'll tell you, folks, other things in life should be this certain.

How to clean your brushes

1 It's important to clean the brush with whatever solvent works with your medium. Here the medium is stain. Rinse with paint thinner.

2 Stick the handle of the brush into the jaws of the trusty paint spinner and spin away. The action of a paint spinner is that of an old-time pump top that kids used to play with. Bbeing a professional allows me to spin in a small jar like you see me doing in the picture because I am well adept at using such a device. Although truth be told, I wasn't able to find anything larger to spin it in and it was the end of the picture shoot anyway, so I said, "What the heck." Usually, though, people will use an empty five-gallon bucket. And honestly, I didn't even knock that jar over once.

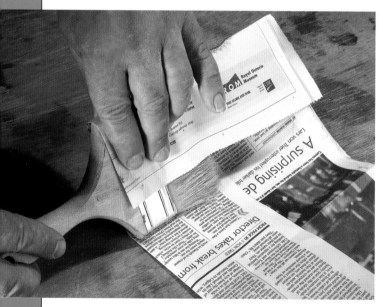

3 After rinsing in the appropriate solvent — and you should do this at least three times with new solvent each time — I wrap the brush in newspaper. This way, I know the brush is going to stay flat.

4 Not much to say here. Nice wrap job, brush looks lonely and, hey, I just noticed while writing this, I think Michael Jackson is on the face of the paper! Look. Completely unintentional I assure you.

The dissolving foam brush

1 Ladies and germs — that is, gentlemen — what you see in my hand is an ordinary made-in-China 2" foam brush. To the right, an ordinary can filled a third full with ordinary lacquer thinner.

2 Uh oh! Someone misplaced the dunking picture but take it from me, I dunked the brush into the lacquer thinner and lo and behold, what do you see? Ladies and gentlemen, look, the brush has somehow gotten bigger and expanded. Wilted from the lacquer bath like a lettuce leaf in hot soup or Joan Rivers in the bathtub. Just imagine, ladies and gentlemen, that you were in the process of brushing a lacquer finish and this happened to you.

3 Side by side, the brush as it was, and after. Turning the book around to read the warning on the wooden handle of the brush — what do we see: NOT FOR SHELLAC OR LACQUER. I thank you.

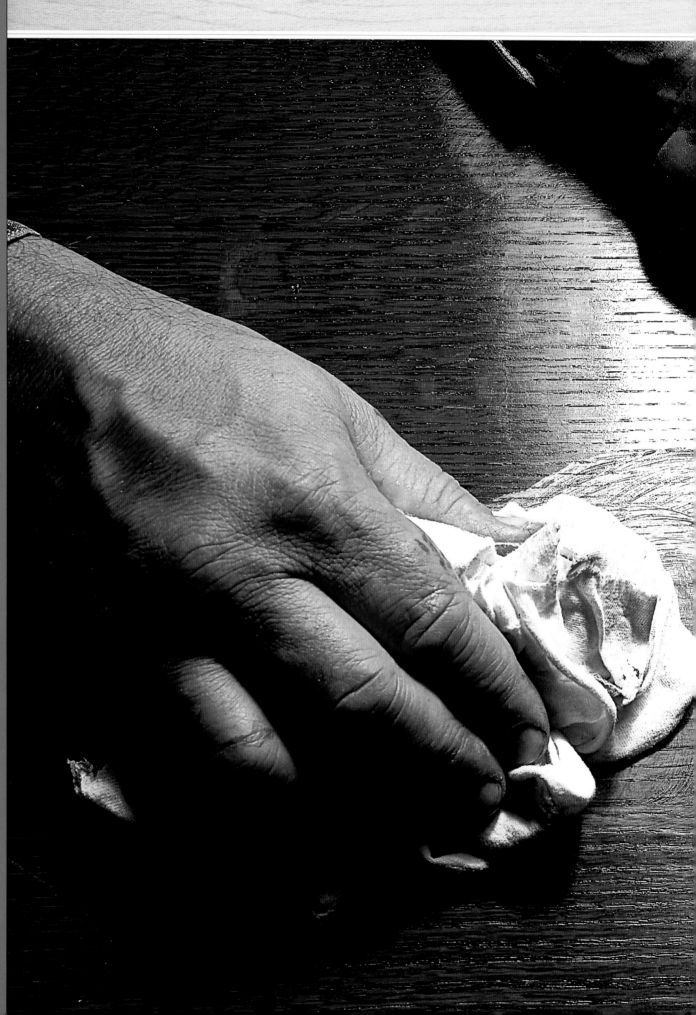

Seven
sure-fire finishes
or limited
shmimited

4

Here's a chance to see, in process, some of the things I've talked about in the last three chapters. You will learn how to make your own wax (just like what I'm holding in my hand), use shoe polish as a final wax, spray finishes without drips and get pickled. Each finish has individual materials lists and specifics on how to use them, bolstered, naturally, by a load of elegant Al Parrish photos.

Limited Shmimited

The result of an any finish rests with ingenuity, and just because there are limitations to buying from the shelf of the home center or paint store doesn't necessarily mean one brown stain and gloss polyurethane — although it does sound like it would make a heck of a finishing-cowboy song, don't it?

My bureau's a wreck and my back is in pain,
Guess I'll saddle ol' Ruthie after brushing her mane,
Makin' a list — get some brushes and stain,
"To the general store" says my wife yet a-Gain,
Go get me one brown stain and gloss poly-UrE-Thane.
OK, so Hank Williams I'm not.

What follows are seven finishes that I've already made reference to as well as materials lists and the specifics on how to achieve them.

Watco and Wax

In a Pickle

Strictly Stickley

Poplar and Walnut

My Cabinet has the Blues

Albert's "Bar Job" Stain

Simple Shellac and Wax

Simple shellac and wax

Shellac and wax is probably the most basic of all finishes. Little time, little effort, nice effect. Keep in mind most of your effort should go into the preparation of the wood — making the wood as smooth as possible through sanding — otherwise, it's like brushing varnish on the trunk of a tree with the hope of achieving a smooth finish. (You thought I was going to say trunk of an elephant didn't you? Which, theoretically would have to be sanded as well and I don't think the elephant would like that.)

The paneling and crown moulding you see in the pictures on the facing page are pine. Both were bought from the home center, installed and sanded to 400-grit sandpaper. After brushing the dust from the wood I applied a spit (a thin sealer) coat of orange shellac (photo 1).

SIMPLE SHELLAC AND WAX

Materials

Amber (orange)
    or Clear (white) Shellac
Denatured alcohol
Bristle brush

Glass or plastic container
320-grit silicon carbide paper
Paste wax
Paper towels

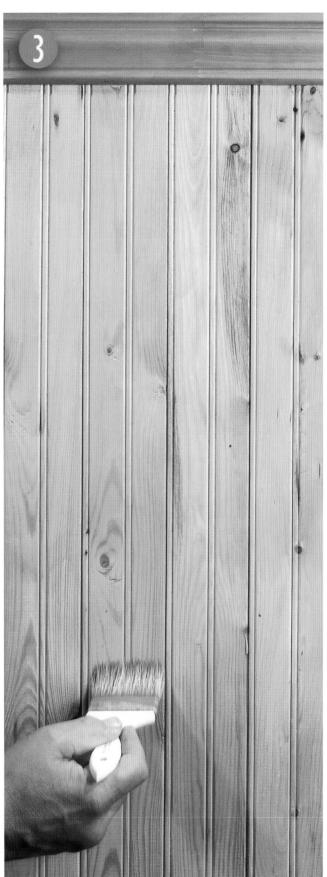

Once the shellac had dried I sanded with 320-grit silicon carbide sandpaper.

I applied a second coat of shellac.

4 I sanded again when the shellac was dry and buffed the finish with No.0000 steel wool.

5 I then waxed the wood with a natural (beeswax) homemade wax and buffed it up. No sweat.

Tips

Oiled finishes

Oiled finishes will repel water quite well. Remember to discard any oil-soaked rags in a bucket of water.

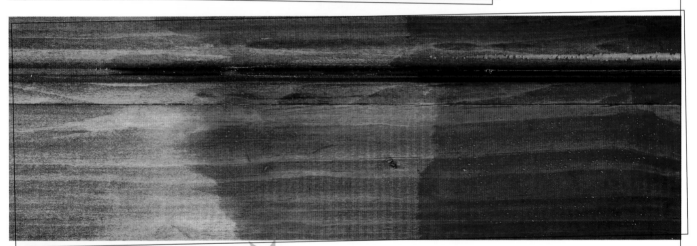

Polyurethane polyshades

The photo above shows a hunk of pine baseboard. The wood was stained first with an oil-based walnut stain and then allowed to dry. When dry, a coat of Minwax polyshade was brushed on. The center area displays this application while the right side reveals the luster a second application of the same polyshade can create.

Consider polyshades akin to washing your head with a shampoo/conditioner in one bottle. Are you really that much in a hurry that you can't first, shampoo, rinse and then condition? Besides, most hair authorities say 2-in-1 step shampoos are not as good as doing one and then the other. I'm telling you that staining your wood first, allowing it to dry and then applying a polyshade for added depth of color and luster is better than any 2-in-1-step anything.

The photo at left shows what can easily happen when using polyshades on a vertical surface. If it runs, it's not good.

Homemade wax

Wax serves a finish as a protective barrier between any spills and the finish itself. Wax is also what great-grandma used before the era of spray polishes (you know as little as ten years ago I could have said grandma, but since these kinds of sprays have been around for some time now, I think I have to use great-grandma) to protect her wood.

There are all types of polishes and waxes on the shelves, most are superior than what was available, say, twenty years ago, and they are there for the taking — as long as you pay for them! But if you would like to make your own wax, it's easier than making a peanut butter sandwich.

Beeswax can be found in industrial hardware stores in the plumbing section where it is known as plumber's wax. You can buy it in pound blocks, which is what I am shaving in the picture. Candles may also be made of beeswax. Shave up as much as you like.

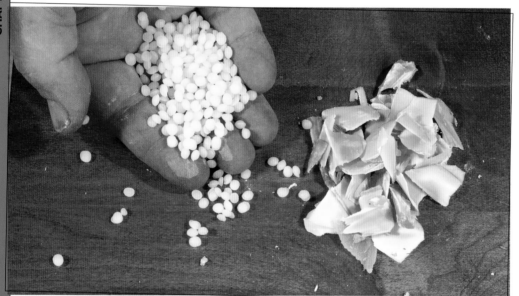

If you prefer, you can purchase these tiny beads of pure beeswax at the art supply store that come packaged in one-pound bags.

Place the shaved or bought beads of wax in a jar and cover the wax with paint thinner or turpentine and allow it to sit overnight.

In the morning, give it a stir and you will see that it has turned into a thick paste indistinguishable from Dream Whip dessert topping. Yum!

Coloring your homemade wax

If the wax I made on the opposite page is easier than making a peanut butter sandwich, coloring the wax would be easier than filling a pot with water.

This is the same wax from the other page, even the same container, into which I am adding a bit of burnt umber dry pigment.

No, it's not fudge, cake batter or chocolate mousse. It's my own homemade colored wax. I even stirred it with my finger.

The advantage of colored wax, especially where dark-colored finishes are concerned, is that it will fill in and cover minor surface scratches. Natural-colored wax products on dark wood will often dry lighter-colored in cracks and crevices and does not look at all attractive.

On the other hand, you can see what happened to the piece of oak I am applying the dark wax to in the picture. After sanding the wood, I used a wire brush to remove the dust from the pores. Rubbing the wax over the wood causes the wax to be pushed into the pores, while at the same time laying down a light amount of color on the wood.

Watco oil and wax

I touched on Watco earlier — and I can still smell it!

There's no doubt that of the major olfactory recollections in my brain, Watco is third only to turpentine and shellac. And although I haven't used the finish for maybe twenty years, I chose to re-create it here because, well, to be honest, it all came back to me when I saw the product on the shelf. I then remembered Ed Fink, the guy I worked for, birch, the endless sanding, the ripped rotator cuff, and the pair of jeans I had to keep in their own container because they smelled so much of Watco. Anywhere I went with those Watco-smelling jeans my ex-wife was able to find me —wherever I was — just by following the trail of aroma.

All you need for this finish is sandpaper, Watco oil and strong elbows. I am using the Watco Natural oil. Fink always had me use the natural oil on birch plywood, which he had usually edge-banded with two- or three-inch solid birch or solid-maple strips. I usually finished the outside and inside in the same way — which is how I tore my rotator cuff.

Let me explain; me on ladder, ladder not at all tall enough, me trying to sand oil into the top underside of the inside of a nine-foot armoire, arm over my head and stretching backwards clutching a monster of an orbital sander that probably weighed about as much as a gallon of milk.

Clear picture?

But enough. The finish is as basic as can be and like the shellac and wax, the prep sanding is paramount to the success of this finish as well.

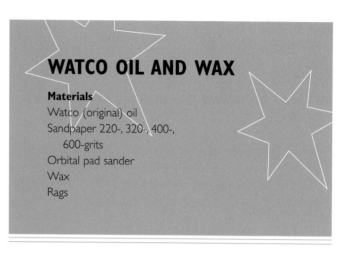

WATCO OIL AND WAX

Materials
Watco (original) oil
Sandpaper 220-, 320-, 400-,
   600-grits
Orbital pad sander
Wax
Rags

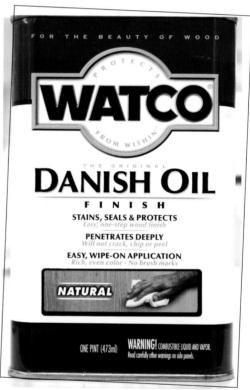

Before the final sanding, wet the wood with a damp cloth, let it dry and final-sand to a maximum smoothness using 400-grit sandpaper.

Apply the oil with a brush or rag and begin sanding.

You can sand by hand or use an orbital sanding machine.

If you want to use an orbital sander to make the Fink finish, you may want to invest in a machine you can use for just Watco — or, even better — use the sander you now own for oiling and buy yourself a new one for all other sanding.

Each time you finish-sand the oil into the wood, wipe away the residue from the surface before applying more oil and sanding with the next higher grit. If you are sanding plywood, know when to stop before you wear through the veneer (see Chapter 3).

Once you have achieved the smoothness and sheen you are looking for, wipe the residue from all surfaces and allow the Watco to dry overnight — then apply the wax of your choice.

Albert's "bar job" finish

The finish for this job was achieved using the signcraft red and burnt umber Ronan Japan colors I talked about earlier. I've substituted artist's oil colors to show you that anything can be changed to achieve the same effect when you have the know-how.

I've known Albert a long time. Albert makes things. I mentioned him in the wood section. Remember? I said he collected walnut. I compared him to a squirrel collecting nuts? Recently, Albert decided to get back into the business of driving himself crazy by making himself available to clients who need things built and he has successfully gotten himself there in no time. Before he was able to pull his shop together, he got a job of building a 29' bar section for a new restaurant that would be opening in South Philadelphia. Naturally, Albert called me in to solve the problem of finishing as the new woods — birch, maple and poplar — had to match the color of an original 80-year-old backbar that would be sitting on top of the new backbar base cabinet he was going to build. Also, there was to be 29' of wraparound raised-panel oak bar which would need to be matched to the color of the old fixture.

I looked at the finish of the old wood for a long time. There was a lot of undercolor present in that old finish that screamed ORANGE!

After experimenting with all different types of coloring agents, and, taking into consideration that I needed to make the entire process as simple as possible because there was a lot of area that needed to be covered (and the clear topcoat was going to have to be brushed on), I was going to need something that would give me the color in two steps, no more. I worked with oil stains, mixing two or three together. One recipe got me close to where I wanted to be but took four steps. I didn't want to use aniline dyes or NGRs (non-grain-raising stains) because I was going to need to sandwich colors by using shellac. Anilines and NGRs are both alcohol-based, so that was no good. After a night of lost sleep, I went to the shop and came across a can of Signcraft red Japan color in my cabinet. This red is orange, well, vermilion would be more exact. From the dried drips on the outside of the can I knew it was the exact undercolor I was looking for. From there, all else followed suit and I've outlined it here for your pleasure.

Once the wood has been sanded, apply your foundation color.

Note: Never sand wood so smooth that the stain will not enter the wood. Wood that has been sanded using a high grit (320 or above) won't absorb the stain well. For oak, no more than 100-grit is necessary unless you want to oil or do a natural finish with oil and wax, vanish or lacquer — then by all means go as high in sanding grits as you like.

Because I am working with a small sample for these pictures, I only had to squeeze out a bit of the artist's oil color onto my disposable pallet. After first dipping my brush into a bit of paint thinner, I dip the bristles of the brush into the glob of paint to thin it (photo 1).

ALBERT'S "BAR JOB" FINISH

Materials
Signcraft red Japan color or artist's oil
Burnt umber Japan color or artist's oil
Orange shellac
Bristle brushes 2"
Plastic containers
320- and 400-grit silicon carbide paper
Brushing lacquer or varnish

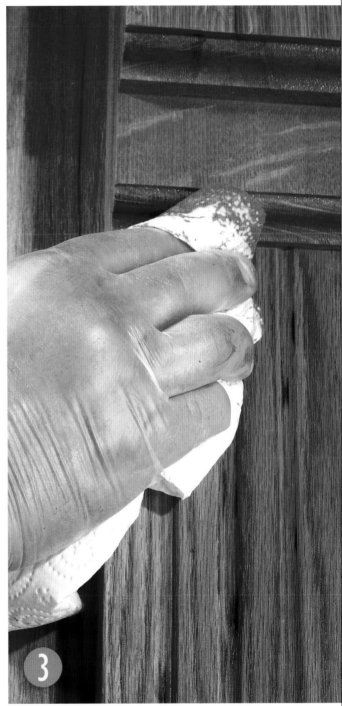

I apply the color to the wood (photo 2) and wipe away the excess with a paper towel (photo 3). After I had applied the initial orange color, I called Albert that night to warn him. When he opened the bay doors to his shop in the morning, I didn't want him to scream and pass out from the effect. When he did see it he said, "Looks like a pumpkin!" And that it did — as you can plainly see. Imagine 29' of this color standing 4' high in your shop!

Once the foundation color had dried, I brushed on a sealer coat of orange shellac (photo 4). All the flat sections of the wood were then lightly sanded using 320-grit silicon carbide sandpaper (photo 5).

The top color was then applied. I used burnt umber artist's tube colors in place of the burnt umber Japan color. I thinned the tube color with mineral spirits the same way I did the orange color. Remember, because you have sealed the first coat of color with the shellac sealer, you can apply a coat of oil-based color without fear of the second color pulling off the first color.

After removing the excess of burnt umber, the stain was allowed to dry.

Next, I brushed on yet another sealer coat of orange shellac.

When the shellac had dried, I sanded lightly with 320-grit sandpaper.

Notice how I have folded the paper to lightly sand the flutes of the pilaster. After dusting and tack-ragging, you can top coat with lacquer or varnish. Do not use polyurethane because it will not adhere to the shellac.

The final finish was a deep, rich color that perfectly matched the old bar finish.

French polishing tampon

Although I do not, and never have considered myself a French polisher, I do know the basics and have performed open-pore French polishing on my share of things. Whereas true French polishing can take many laborious hours of rubbing to achieve what many consider to be the ultimate look — applying coat after coat of shellac, pumice and paraffin oil until you have one giant arm like Popeye, open-pore French polishing is quickly laid down and may be considered a prelude to beginning to learn the art of French polishing.

First thing you need to know is how to make a polishing *tampon* or applicator. The core of the tampon is wool. In my hands are two types of wool. On the left, a wool sock I cut up, and, on the right, some actual wool I got from a sheep when he wasn't looking.

I dipped the piece of wool into some 2-pound-cut shellac and then squeezed the juice out of it. The wool, being absorbent like a sponge, holds its own.

You don't want it soaking wet and neither do you want it completely dry.

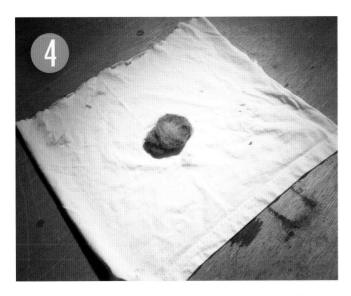

Lay the wool in the center of a 12" × 12" piece of trace cloth or an old white undershirt. The idea is to trap it in the cloth and fold it so that it can fit neatly and comfortably in your palm. (Here's where you need to experiment, because you need to discover exactly how much cloth your particular polishing paw is going to need. It all depends on the size of your hand. For me it's 12" square, but if your hands are smaller you may only need 8" square — Andre the Giant could have used an entire pillow case when he set out to French polish!)

Fold one end over into the middle, then another...

...and another and another. When you have all four corners folded in where the tips meet in the middle, fold inward again.

You'll wind up with a smaller square, with the wool trapped within, directly under where my finger is holding down the points of the ends.

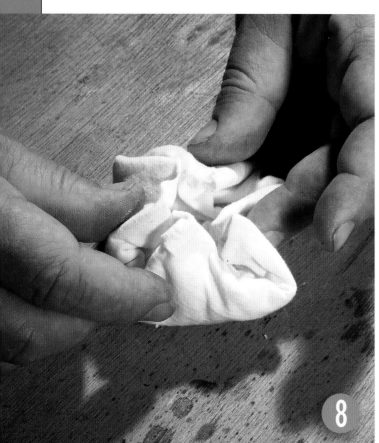

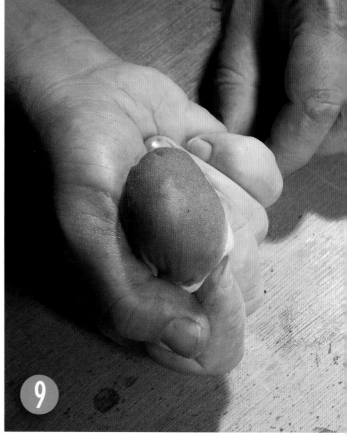

Now, the trick is to squeeze and twist the cloth with the wool in the center so that it may be gathered together.

The end result is what you see here. It's comfortable in my hand with absolutely no excess of cloth. An excess of cloth whipping around as you move can be a real bother once the application of shellac starts.

Applying shellac to the pad is accomplished by pouring the liquid onto the pad while holding the pad as shown in photo 9. While I prefer to fill brown glass bottles with my shellac, plastic squeeze bottles with a pointed tip — like a squeeze ketchup bottle — will do as well.

Once the pad is thoroughly wet and not dripping all over the place, pound the applicator in the open palm of your other hand and then land the pad — as an airplane lands — on the surface of the wood and begin making figure-8 motions around and around and around. As you finish up, or, as the pad begins losing liquid, pull the pad from the surface as an airplane taking off.

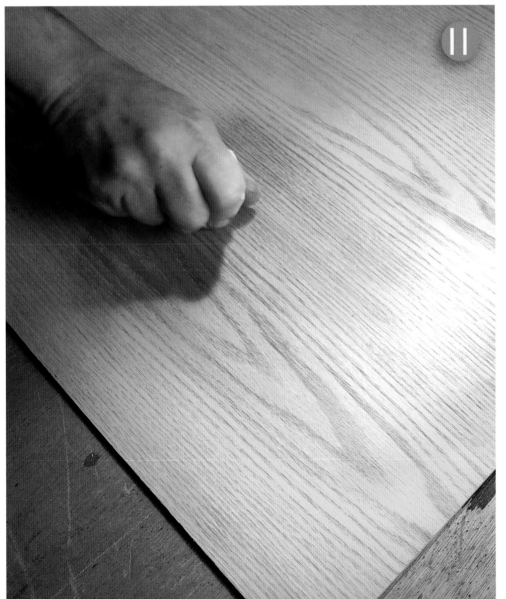

Apply more of your shellac mix to the applicator pad and land again, remembering always to take off when you're ready to leave the surface of the wood — and never rest the pad on the surface after you've begun to build up surface finish. The wet pad will eat into the finish and ruin your work.

You can already see a sheen building in the center of the piece of wood in this photo after a mere two applications. Imagine applying forty-two coats of finish, incorporating pumice (which serves to polish the shellac film as well as filling any pores) into the rub. Now you understand why not too many people are willing to put in the time to learn this granddaddy of all finishes.

In a pickle (whitewash on oak or pine)

IN A PICKLE

Materials
White oil paint
Stain brush
Paper towels
White shellac
Denatured alcohol
Plastic containers
Paste wax

Designers are always wanting to talk about the pickled finish. I can't tell you how many of these of these finishes I've done in my time. Keep in mind, not many designers know the real recipe for the pickled look — which entails using *unslaked lime*. (Try that one on for size! Look it up.)

Usually what designers want (and what you can achieve) is done easily with white paint and solvent or, water, if you're keen on using latex paint.

The effect is best achieved on oak, ash and some types of pine. On oak or ash, the paint will fill the pores as well as render a chalky look to the rest of the wood. With pine the wood will chalk-up, but it's harder to render an even look. If there are mouldings, the paint-wash will gather in the crevices. If this isn't to your liking you can always paint the wood white.

The panel in this example is a red oak plywood panel with solid red oak moulding attached to it.

Red oak, because of it's strong color, will add to the white-washed effect, creating a pink overtone (think Andy Warhol). White oak will have a starker pallor (for those old enough, think Edgar Winter).

After scrubbing the wood lightly with a wire brush (going with the grain as much as you can), apply the thinned white paint.

This is something you mix to your liking. To start, I suggest three or four parts solvent to one part white paint. You may want it thicker, so you would need to reduce the amount of solvent or water (if you're using latex paint). Get it? (Remember, if you are using latex paint, it will raise the grain and the paint will set-up fast — so work quickly.)

It's about feel and achieving the look that you want.

After painting the surfaces, wipe the excess from the wood using paper towels.

If the paint has set-up, wet your wiping towel with thinner and continue the wiping surfaces. The thinner will reactivate the paint and removal will be easier.

If you've used latex paint and it begins to set up before you've had time to remove it evenly, you will have a harder time trying to remove the excess. This is why I always use oil paint for this type of finish.

Wipe the excess paint from the wood, first across the grain and then with the grain. Wiping across the grain will push the paint into the pores and then gently wiping with the grain will even out the look.

Once all surfaces have been washed and wiped, allow everything to dry for twenty-four hours or so.

Apply a coat of white (clear) shellac using a 1-to-5 spit coat.

Sand this sealer coat with 320-grit sandpaper, rub with No. 0000 steel wool and apply a coat of wax. Or, you can top coat with lacquer or Varathane.

Top coating with polyurethane or varnish is not advised because they are amber colored. The white effect could wind up looking old and yellowed. The clearest *water-clear* finish is lacquer. For the novice, I recommend that you use brushing lacquer. You should practice using brushing lacquer on a sample piece first.

Pickled finish on pine

After sanding the wood, dust off and then apply the paint, using the same method as for oak.

Once the wood is covered, you can pull the paint across flat surfaces.

I like to use paper towels to rid the surface of excess paint. This is where it can get tricky. Using uneven pressure when you rub can remove more paint in some areas than in others. You won't have this problem with oak.

Use a soft-hair brush (from the art supply store) to help even out the stain and color.

Strictly, Stickley oak

This is as true a finish as can be. Earlier, I mentioned the Stickley technique of coloring wood by fuming with ammonia gas — which was then shellacked and waxed with black wax to accentuate the grain markings. That's Stickley. With all that ammonia around, you can bet he never found himself falling asleep on the job.

Here is a way to arrive at the same effect while nixing the ammonia fuming, which can rid the nasal passages of, well, their passages!

Replace the coloring agent (80-100% ammonia — hard to find anyway) with artist's oil colors and you're on your way.

This finish will work on solid wood as well as plywood, although if used on plywood, remember to shellac first, utilizing the 1-to-5 ratio of thinned shellac for spit-coat. This will prevent too much absorbtion of color.

STRICTLY STICKLY OAK

Materials
Burnt umber Japan color
Burnt sienna Japan color
Paint thinner
Assorted wire brushes
Black shoe polish
Rags

The wood should be sanded using 80-grit sandpaper. A wire brush is then pulled carefully parallel to the grain, always being careful to not cross the grain. Plywood should be prepped the same as solid wood. Apply the shellac spit coat.

Artist's burnt umber oil color thinned with paint thinner or turpentine is then applied in a circular motion with paper towels or a lint free rag. Move the circles around and around grinding the color into the pores.

Wipe across the grain and finish by wiping with the grain to even the surface of any smears. Allow this to dry for at least 48 hours, or longer if the humidity has been high when applied.

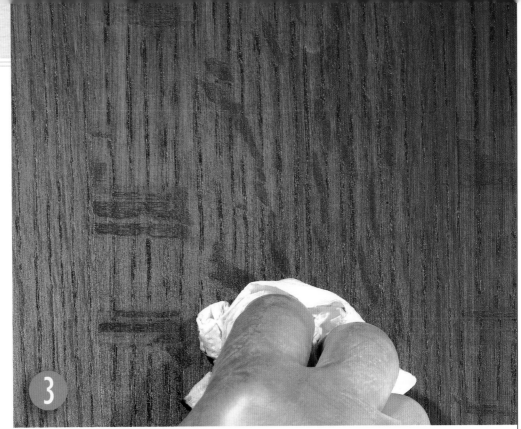

Apply a spit coat of shellac to all surfaces. When dry, sand with 320-grit silicon carbide paper. Then, apply a topcoat of Varathane, varnish or lacquer. Do not use a polyure-thane topcoat.

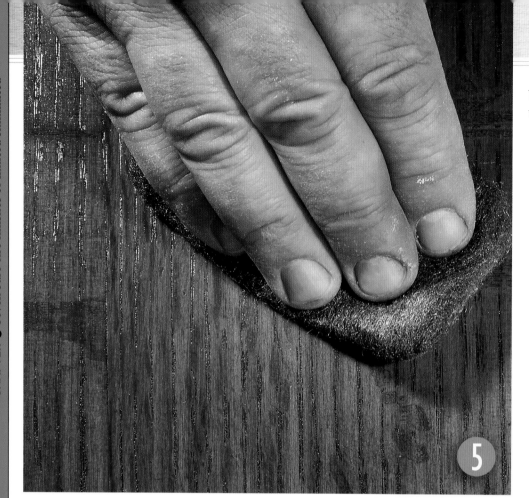

When dry, rub the topcoat using No.0000 steel wool.

Wax all surfaces using black shoe polish (photos 6-8). No foolin'!

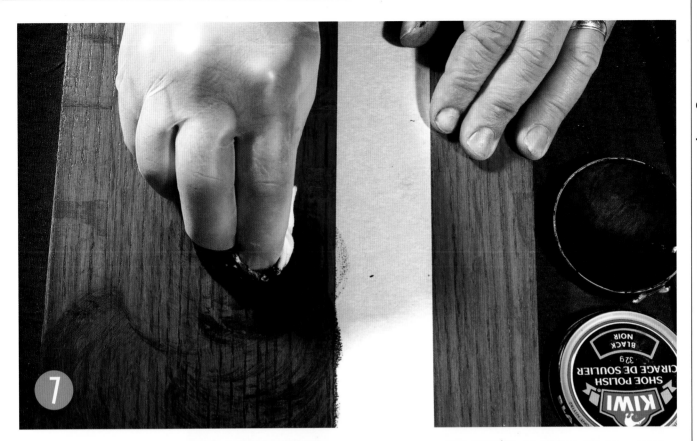

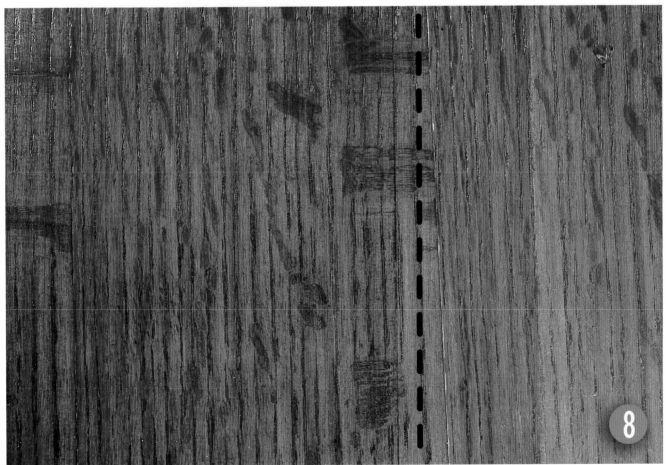

This side with black wax.

Poplar and walnut

No. This technique is not named after the title of the flip side of Paul McCartney and Michael Jackson's hit single, *Ebony and Ivory*.

In woodworking, there are times when you will mix wood species in a single project. That's okay. When you do, and you want to render the woods to match each other, it's important that you know how to fake it. Poplar can be matched to just about any wood with the exception of the open pore woods such as ash, oak and chestnut.

In the United States, I often work for a company that imports bars and backbars from Belgium. The Belgian cabinetmakers will mix old components, such as mahogany or walnut raised panels, with new poplar rails and stiles. Even though the Belgians color them with dark pigment, they always need toning up and matching. When they come into the shop as raw however, I have my work cut out for me.

First I sanded the wood, taped off the walnut from the poplar and applied a thin wash coat of shellac to the poplar — about a 10-to-1 mix. This was applied as a precautionary measure; just in case the wood felt like splotching.

After the shellac dried, I applied a base stain on both sides and allowed it to dry. I used Minwax special walnut oil stain. When dry, I shellacked both sides and let it dry.

POPLAR AND WALNUT

Materials
Burnt umber oil color
Burnt sienna oil color
Black oil color
Paint thinner
Orange shellac
Brushes
Disposable pallet

I sanded the dry shellac with 320-grit silicon carbide sandpaper and then applied a mixture of burnt umber/burnt sienna thinned with paint thinner. Once this was wiped away, I allowed it to dry and shellacked the entire surface.

You may have to re-coat a third time with the burnt umber/burnt sienna mix, but, with a little practice, you'll be able to even out the color and cover things up better than former President Nixon. Remember to shellac the final stain and allow it all to dry before you top coat.

The final, top-coated sample — poplar on the left and walnut on the right. This is a good coloring technique to have in your bag of finishing tricks.

My cabinet has the blues

Paint can be a simple finishing remedy for wood, especially if the wood is pine, which just so happens to be one of the most paintable woods. A cabinet like this is available at craft stores as well as unfinished-furniture stores. I bought this cabinet for peanuts simply because the top had a planer burn running across the top. I took care of the burn with a belt sander and was ready to go.

MY CABINET HAS THE BLUES

Materials
100-grit sandpaper
White spray primer
Permanent Blue Japan color
Blue spray enamel
Masking tape
Newspaper

Anytime you work on something like this, that is, a cabinet with hinges and hardware and such, you want to remove as much of it as possible. In this case, I took off the door, the hinges, the knob and the doorstop.

After sanding everything with 100-grit, I gave all the wood a good shellacking. Any time you are going to paint something, make sure you give it a sealer coat of shellac. This creates a much better surface to paint. Certainly, it's a smoother beginning than brushing paint onto un-shellacked wood.

Once the shellac dries, sand the wood with 320-grit silicon carbide paper and brush all traces of sanding dust from the wood. The idea with this demonstration was to use two shades of blue, not only for effect but to show you two methods of application. So, for the top and the door I selected a royal blue gloss spray enamel, and a permanent blue Japan color for the cabinet case.

After shellacking and sanding all surfaces you must prime the wood. I am using an enamel primer. Notice that I've covered the bottom of the cabinet using masking tape and a skirt of newspaper. No need getting any unnecessary paint on the work — even though the bottom side is going to be painted anyway.

Be sure when you spray that you have a full can of spray paint, this will assure that no spitting occurs. You also need to agitate the paint. This means you gotta shake your can. (May I suggest putting on some James Brown?) Always test the spray. If the spray cone of paint is even flowing, proceed, moving slowly across the surface, 6'- 8" from the wood. Begin at least 2 - 3" off the top before you hit the top and continue for at least 2 - 3" inches after you have passed the end of the top. This way, you will not create a heavy buildup of spray in one spot. (See the illustration.)

Move in a straight line and do not spray with a curve, or pendulum-like motion. This is the most common mistake when spraying with aerosols.

After the primer has dried, sand with 320-grit silicon carbide sandpaper and tack rag. Here, I am applying the blue spray enamel made by the same company as the primer, so I know these are compatible. This is important. If you spray a lacquer over an enamel, the lacquer can bubble the enamel. So not only should you shake your can — you should also read the label.

After the first coat of spray had dried (about 4 hours) I sanded and applied a second coat. I did the same with the door.

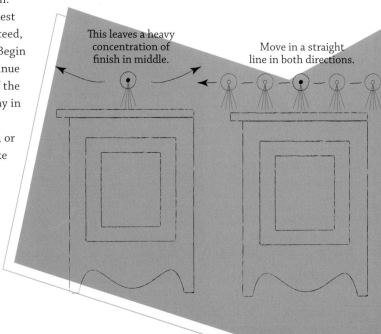

This leaves a heavy concentration of finish in middle.

Move in a straight line in both directions.

Applying the blue Japan color is no different than applying any type of paint straight from the can. You can see that I have the cabinet laying on its back so that I can paint the front face without fear of drips — unless you manage to drip down the sides. I finished the sides in the same way, laying the piece on its left side, allowing it to dry, and then turning the piece to the right side.

After the first coat of Japan color dried, I shellacked all the painted surfaces, sanded with 320-grit silicon carbide sandpaper and then recoated. Because of the flat luster this type of paint offers, I opted to leave it uncoated. I think the flat finish balances the gloss of the top and door.

I think the cabinet looks wonderful in my yard right next to my wife's hydrangea. Whaddaya think?

Method for spraying or brushing on the level

There is a sure-fire way to prevent drips. Whenever you spray or brush varnish, polyurethane or lacquer on a piece of furniture, you're going to get drips.

When brushing a finish on wood that's built in, be it baseboard or a wall unit, you run the risk of runs on the wood.

I'm so good at brushing I was able to manage only one drip (see photo 7, page 87) and, I have to be honest, it took a while to get that drip to do that!

But there's no reason for this to happen when you brush finish on a piece of furniture because, unless you're finishing or painting a Trojan Horse or Howard Hughes' Spruce Goose, typical indoor furniture has two sides, a front and a top and the piece can be maneuvered.

You have the power to move the furniture piece. You can do it alone, but it's better if you invite friends over to help. Remember to take your time and do one part or section at a time.

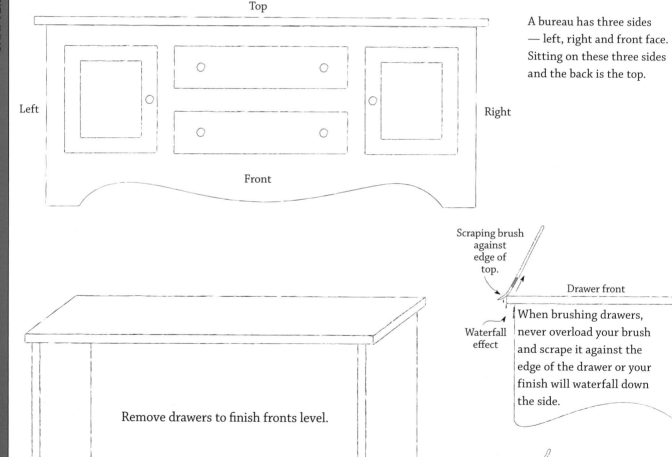

Top

Left

Right

Front

A bureau has three sides — left, right and front face. Sitting on these three sides and the back is the top.

Scraping brush against edge of top.

Drawer front

Waterfall effect

When brushing drawers, never overload your brush and scrape it against the edge of the drawer or your finish will waterfall down the side.

Remove drawers to finish fronts level.

Stop tip of bristles at edge.

Drawer front

You should brush right up to the edge, but only to the tip of the bristles and not over the edge.

Before handling the casework, pull all of the drawers out and remove any doors and hardware. Stand the drawers up and lay the doors flat. This will allow you to brush or spray them on the level.

Paint only to edges of top.

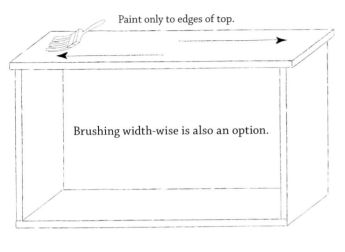

Brushing width-wise is also an option.

Lift the piece so it sits on the right side, which will allow you to coat the left side so that it will dry level.

Turning a piece up on end means you may have to block it up as tops often extend over the sides and will prevent the piece from sitting level.

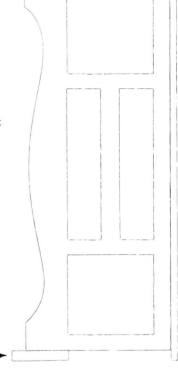

Leveling block ➝

Lay flat to do front face.

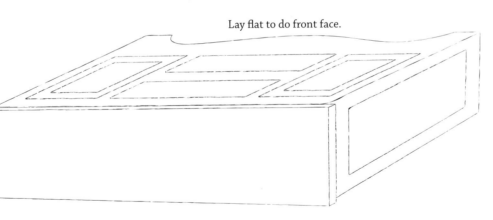

Once the side has dried (at least 24 hrs), turn the piece over and stand it on the newly finished side. Place some cardboard on the floor topped with a layer of wax paper and proceed with your application of finish. When both sides have been finished, lay the piece on its back and apply finish to the front.

Last but not least, finish the top.

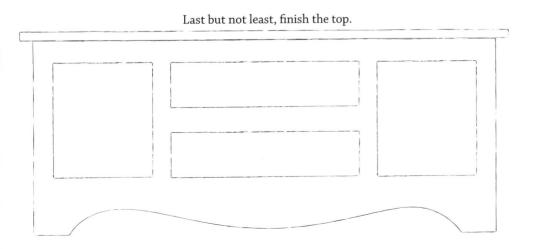

Rubbing out and polishing a finish

Rubbing out a finish is not something that is done much these days. In fact, you may find, on certain labels of cans of clear finish, the notice: *gives that hand-rubbed look* — but what does this mean? And how can it give that look without having been hand rubbed? Most people seem to think a finish doesn't have to be rubbed out, or that rubbing out is an unnecessary step — three coats of lacquer or varnish on the wood and that's that. But, if you've already gone that far (especially on a top surface), why wouldn't you want the finish to feel and look as good as it can? One thing to remember, if you are considering rubbing out a finish, is to always use *gloss* lacquer or varnish. Satin and semigloss finishes contain flattening agents (talc) that produce low-luster results. When a satin or semigloss surface is rubbed out, it will feel smoother but it won't have that rubbed-out and polished mirror finish.

To rub out a final coat of finish, start by wet sanding with the grain using 320-grit silicon carbide paper (photo 1). Either plain or soapy water can be used. This step will eliminate any dust that may have settled and become trapped during drying time. Rub evenly across the surface, using steady pressure. Be careful of edges where you might break through and expose the wood under the stain and finish. When the paper starts sticking to the wood through suction, you will need to change paper. You can wrap sandpaper around a felt block to wet sand if you like, or just use your hand on the paper.

The white on my fingertips is the abraded finish, combined with residue from the silicon carbide paper (photo 2).

After wet sanding, clean the surface of all the gray powdery residue with water and paper towels. For the next step, I use No.0000 steel wool. For small areas, a pad the size of a shredded-wheat biscuit can be torn into three equal-sized pieces and rolled in the hands to make smaller pads. Small pads are good for rubbing the edges, carvings or mouldings. Like sandpaper, steel wool clogs and needs to be discarded when you feel it's not cutting.

Unfolding two or three pads and sandwiching them together can make larger rolls of steel wool for rubbing-out top surfaces. When you see traces of dust on the bottom of the pad, the pad will stop cutting and polishing the finish. This means it's time to unfold the pad and then roll it tightly again, exposing a new area of clean wool.

Keep an even pressure on the wool as you rub (photo 3). Be cautious when polishing shellac. The heat generated by the friction of rubbing can soften the shellac and damage the finish.

After you're done polishing the finish with the steel wool, clean the surface with a soft cloth. (You'll know you're done polishing with the steel wool when the entire finish is shiny.)

If you want to go another step after using the steel wool, you can use pumice and rotten-stone with water to further polish the finish. Pumice (on the block of wood to the left) is powered volcanic ash and comes in grits from 1F to 4F, 1F being the coarsest. Rottenstone is decomposed limestone that is a gray color (on the block of wood to the right). Both of these may be used with water or mineral oil to further abrade and polish the finish. I learned to do this step using these traditional abrasives, but by today's standards, they are outmoded. Car polishing compounds offer the same effect with much less aggravation.

When the polishing with the compounds is done, apply a coat of Butcher (amber) wax or Minwax dark wax, depending on the color of your finish.

If you've done a good job, you should be able to see yourself. It will take some practice for you to master the art of rubbing out a finish. But, the reward will be great, especially when you place a cold drink on the table and see its reflection — but don't forget to use a coaster, you animal!

Questions and Answers

DEDICATION

To the memory of George Frank, master cabinetmaker and wood finisher, who first inspired and revealed to me the true art and wonder of wood finishing. And to my wife, Heidi, for her faith, love, and understanding my mentioning her after Mr. Frank.

George Frank

I often buy wood at the local home center and always have a problem removing those darn bar code stickers. I mean, I think I've removed them, but then I put finish on and sometimes (most times!) I still see the outline. Relax. This has happened to me as well. The problem with any sticker, which is why we call them "stickers", is that they are bound by adhesives and, well, stick! Adhesive residue and the stickers can removed with paint thinner.

Usually, I wet some cotton or a paper towel with paint thinner and lay it on the sticker. Give the lacquer thinner a bit of time to seep through the paper, then it's a matter of scrapping away the sticker and adhesive with a single-edge razor blade.

I found an old can of oil stain in my shop cabinet and applied it to a desk I made. It's been a week and the stain is still tacky. What do I do? Old stains, new problems. Whenever you're not sure how old a product is, it's usually better to go out and purchase something new. As for the stain not drying, chances are the driers have evaporated, leaving more of a sludge than a stain.

I would recommend washing down the wood with paint thinner several times — using new thinner each time. Allow the wood to dry and then wash the wood with alcohol. Next, go out and buy a new stain.

I have made several cabinets with different sizes of drawers and, while the drawers always seem to work before finishing, they always seem to stick afterwards. The sides of the drawers may have the same amount of finish on them as the piece of furniture. This can be one problem. You are creating friction with the addition of too much finish.

The other problem can be the wood (before and after applying finish) has swelled. First, I would try rubbing on some wax, such as an old candle, paraffin (used for preserving jams and jellies) or a bar of soap. Take the candle remnant, block of wax or bar of soap and rub the bottom edges of the sides of the drawers until you are indenting the wax and you can see a thick deposit of wax or soap left on the wood. Now, insert the drawer and push it in and pull it out until it functions properly.

You may have to repeat this process every now and again. Of course, you can go a step further in your construction and employ drawer glides.

How many coats of finish should I apply to my wood working project?

That would depend on the project. I had a friend who made organic figurative sculptures out of cherry and walnut, and, after sanding the heck out of them, would apply up to fifteen coats of polyurethane. Normally, on a piece of furniture, when you are brushing on a varnish, polyurethane or lacquer, three coats is sufficient.

I recently purchased brushing lacquer and have had a hard time applying my second and third coats. Why?

Lacquer is a solvent-release finish, which means the solvent evaporates and what's left behind is a dry film. When you apply a second coat of lacquer — especially when brushing — that second coat is going to eat into the first one. This is essentially is the way lacquer and shellac, another solvent-release finish, bond.

Knowing this, the secret is in being adept with the brush and knowing your material. The other essential thing to know is that, unlike varnish or polyurethane, which can be applied willy-nilly, lacquer requires a special technique. (Willy-nilly is the only way I know to describe what I'm trying to say. There is an order to the way I apply paint, varnish or polyurethane, unlike the way you may see a homeowner applying paint to a wall on one of the many decorating shows on television. With the homeowner's brush going every-which-way, because they've never painted before in their lives, let alone held a brush, this is willy-nilly, get it?)

My order for applying paint, varnish or polyurethane to a section of raised paneling would be to do the panels first and then tie in the rails and stiles. My method for applying brushing lacquer however, would be to brush from the top of the panel to the bottom of the panel, moving from left to right until I reach the end.

Using this method, I won't brush over the finish I have already laid down. I hope this is clear enough. If not, wait for the next book!

I build things mainly from pine and would like to know how I can age the wood. I've tried applying dark oil stains but haven't found a way to fool anyone yet. Fake! FAKE! You mean people are out there who would try and fake others?

Naturally, I jest. People have been making fakes for years, and, I've done my share of creating fake-antique finishes. If you have a clear visual sense of what old things look like, you will have half the battle won. Generally, I have used lye to age wood. Mix a can of Red Devil lye in a gallon of hot water and then slather it over old pine boards. This will change them dramatically. The boards may even be beaten up first with chains, rocks, gravel — whatever you like. Be sure to sand off any sharp tears and burrs. Rasps may be used for wearing away corners.

To neutralize the lye, wash the boards with a mixture of one part white vinegar to one part water. All that's left to do is color over the lye. I've used Japan colors (page 75) with great success. Apply a sealer-coat of shellac, then either varnish or wax.

The choices are many, but as I said, it's important to having a clear sense of what old things look like — like Billy Crystal these days!

I would like to know what kind of finish would be non-toxic for kid's stuff. I once made a cradle out of ash. (The plans called for pine, but I didn't have pine so I used ash.) Since the cradle was for my son, I wanted something as non-toxic as possible. I settled for a burnished finish coated in paraffin wax.

Burnishing is a means by which one compresses the fibers of the wood until they become shiny. Ash is a perfect candidate for this process because the wood is dense. If you have ever gone up a staircase and felt a banister that appeared to be smooth and sleek but were unable to detect a finish, that banister will have been burnished from many hands holding onto it while ascending and descending. In effect, the wood was smoothed by the friction and the oils of people's flesh. This takes many years occur, and so, to speed up this process, what I had to do was to get the wood of the cradle as smooth as possible. I sanded up to 400-grit sandpaper. Each time I changed grits I wetting the wood to raise the grain and then sanding the raised grain smooth. Once the wood felt as smooth as silk, I began the laborious process of burnishing.

Burnishing can be achieved with chrome implements or bone — ivory being one of the old-time burnishing tools, but few elephants these days are willing to donate to the trade. What one does is rub the wood until the fibers compress and the wood becomes shinny. For my burnishing tools I used the chrome edges of different sizes of ratchet wrenches, burnishing tools I purchased from the art supply store and, for the larger surfaces, I was able to locate the chrome back from an old ice cream parlor seat (the kind that used to swivel and squeak when you turned in them).

This back looked like an old-time saw with two handles, and, the magical part was that the back was concentric, that is, it was formed to fit the human back. I used this to rub the sides and top canopy, the back and the front, while the edges were burnished using the other implements.

Once the entire cradle's surface was smooth and silky, I melted some paraffin wax in a double boiler (one can, partially filled with water, and another that fits into it, filled with the shaved wax). Once the wax had melted, I painted it quickly onto the sides, back, front and canopy, making sure to cover all edges. This wax coating, which kind of looked like icing on a cake, was then carefully scrapped off using different kinds of scrappers. Then the fun part came. I had to rid the wood surfaces of any trace of irregular wax deposits. To do this, I rubbed the heck out of it with wads of burlap. The heat of the friction from my rubbing removed just what I wanted it to (I'm huffing just remembering it all).

It's a lot of work, true, but let me tell you, the effect is beautiful — and non-toxic.

I've heard a lot about filling the pores of the wood before applying finish. Is this necessary?

Nothing in finishing is really necessary except that you follow the rules. Filling pores is done so the resulting surface finish is completely level and mirror-like. This is fine if that's what you're after. Most high-end furniture is filled and lacquered. More basic, rustic furniture is not. It's a look and nothing more.

Wood filler has a mineral spirit (paint thinner) base and is thick like pudding. It is applied with a brush across the grain and then the excess is wiped off briskly with burlap, first across the grain and then with the grain. The surface must dry for twenty-four hours and can then be sealed. The sealer coat is sanded and then recoated as many times as you like. Since the pores have been filled, the varnish or lacquer will not sink into them. The result is a smooth, mirror-like finish. Ta-da!

Suppliers

Adams & Kennedy — The Wood Source
6178 Mitch Owen Rd.
P.O. Box 700
Manotick, ON
Canada K4M 1A6
613-822-6800
www.wood-source.com
Wood supply

Adjustable Clamp Company
404 N. Armour St.
Chicago, IL 60622
312-666-0640
www.adjustableclamp.com
Clamps and woodworking tools

B&Q
Portswood House
1 Hampshire Corporate Park
Chandlers Ford
Eastleigh
Hampshire, England SO53 3YX
0845 609 6688
www.diy.com
Woodworking tools, supplies and hardware

Busy Bee Tools
130 Great Gulf Dr.
Concord, ON
Canada L4K 5W1
1-800-461-2879
www.busybeetools.com
Woodworking tools and supplies

Constantine's Wood Center of Florida
1040 E. Oakland Park Blvd.
Fort Lauderdale, FL 33334
800-443-9667
www.constantines.com
Tools, woods, veneers, hardware

Frank Paxton Lumber Company
5701 W. 66th St.
Chicago, IL 60638
800-323-2203
www.paxtonwood.com
Wood, hardware, tools, books

The Home Depot
2455 Paces Ferry Rd. NW
Atlanta, GA 30339
800-430-3376 (U.S.)
800-628-0525 (Canada)
www.homedepot.com
Woodworking tools, supplies and hardware

Klingspor Abrasives Inc.
2555 Tate Blvd. SE
Hickory, N.C. 28602
800-645-5555
www.klingspor.com
Sandpaper of all kinds

Lee Valley Tools Ltd.
P.O. Box 1780
Ogdensburg, NY 13669-6780
800-871-8158 (U.S.)
800-267-8767 (Canada)
www.leevalley.com
Woodworking tools and hardware

Lowe's Companies, Inc.
P.O. Box 1111
North Wilkesboro, NC 28656
800-445-6937
www.lowes.com
Woodworking tools, supplies and hardware

Mohawk Finishing Products
Division of RPM Wood
Finishes Group, Inc.
P.O. Box 22000
Hickory, NC 28603-0220
800-545-0047
www.mohawk-finishing.com
Touch-up markers, fillers, epoxy adhesives and a complete line of kits and repair products for wood, leather and vinyl

Rockler Woodworking and Hardware
4365 Willow Dr.
Medina, MN 55340
800-279-4441
www.rockler.com
Woodworking tools, hardware and books

Trend Machinery & Cutting Tools Ltd.
Odhams Trading Estate
St. Albans Rd.
Watford
Hertfordshire, U.K.
WD24 7TR
01923 224657
www.trendmachinery.co.uk
Woodworking tools and hardware

Waterlox Coatings
9808 Meech Ave.
Cleveland, OH 44105
800-321-0377
www.waterlox.com
Finishing supplies

Woodcraft Supply, L.L.C.
1177 Rosemar Rd.
P.O. Box 1686
Parkersburg, WV 26102
800-535-4482
www.woodcraft.com
Woodworking hardware

Woodworker's Hardware
P.O. Box 180
Sauk Rapids, MN 56379-0180
800-383-0130
www.wwhardware.com
Woodworking hardware

Woodworker's Supply
1108 N. Glenn Rd.
Casper, WY 82601
800-645-9292
http://woodworker.com
Woodworking tools and accessories, finishing supplies, books and plans

Index

More great titles from Popular Woodworking!

THE WOODWORKER'S BIBLE
By Percy W. Blandford

This book covers everything the woodworker needs to know about woodworking tools, how to equip a basic tool kit and how to use and care for hand tools and power tools. There are chapters on wood fasteners, wood joints, wood lathes, carving and whittling, veneering and inlaying and how to choose the correct finish for your projects.

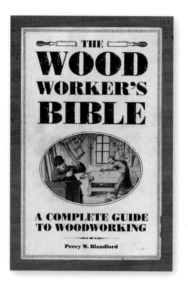

ISBN 13: 978-1-55870-826-6
ISBN 10: 1-55870-826-X
hardcover, 416 p., #Z1553

WORKBENCHES
By Christopher Schwarz

This is the only workbench book that shows you how to design a good workbench, how to build it and most importantly how to use it in your shop for all sorts of tasks. And it shows you how to use this knowledge to design a workbench for the ages, using two venerable designs as basic skeletons.

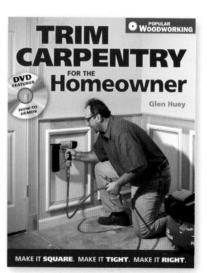

ISBN 13: 978-1-55870-840-2
ISBN 10: 1-55870-840-5
hardcover, 144 p., # Z1981

HAND TOOL ESSENTIALS
From the editors of Popular Woodworking magazine

This book is about using hand tools in balance with your power tools to save you time, provide a more pleasant workworking experience and ultimately give you a better woodworking project. You'll learn how to choose and use hand tools for chopping, cutting, paring, sawing, marking, drilling and more.

ISBN 13: 978-1-55870-815-0
ISBN 10: 1-55870-815-4
paperback, 224 p., # Z0978

TRIM CARPENTRY FOR THE HOMEOWNER
By Glen Huey

This book contains:
• Design advice
• Detailed instruction on installing or replacing door, window and other room trims, such as chair moulding.
• Step-by-step information about fireplace surrounds, mantels, wainscoting and built-in furniture.

Also included is a DVD with detailed instructions.

ISBN 13: 978-1-55870-814-3
ISBN 10: 1-55870-814-6
paperback w/DVD, 128 p., # Z0953